What they're saying about
Weathering the Storm

Amidst the chaos and dysfunction of a life scarred by abuse, neglect, and hurt, Phyllis shares with such transparency, the effects heartache and turmoil had in her life. Searching for love and acceptance, she found herself vulnerable and involved in empty relationships. When nothing else would fill her void, she would turn to drugs, only to be driven to a deeper place of desperation. In her darkest moment, thinking there was no way out, she thought about taking her life, but GOD intervened and made a way for her.

Phyllis and her precious baby girl entered the program at New Life Home, where God began to heal and rebuild her life. Throughout the months, I watched God transform her heart and mind. "Old things were passed away, and everything became new." Slowly but surely, this beautiful young woman began to see herself as God saw her.

God had a plan for her life. It was evident God had His hand upon her life and was preparing her for His purposes. Throughout the years, I have watched Phyllis go through the most trying and difficult times, but God has sustained her through it all. Her trust is in the Lord is evident as she has embarked in steps of faith, ministering to those who are hurting, imprisoned, and bound.

Her life is a testimony to the power of God not only to save but to sustain and empower us to become victorious through Him.

GRACE ROSADO
Co-Founder and Executive Director, New Life Home
for Women & Children, Manchester, New Hampshire

From the moment I met Phyllis, I knew there was something different about her. She had a passion for prayer and a presence—especially in prayer—that I had not known before. Phyllis is a prayer warrior. When she called for volunteers for a ministry she worked for, I felt drawn to join her. There was a spiritual connection. Working with her in ministry was a blessing to me in my early years in the faith. She was effective at bringing the message of the gospel and the saving grace of Jesus Christ to women in need. I saw lives change. Phyllis is anointed for this work. The Holy Spirit moves within her, stirring her and effectively moving those in her care toward healing. Working with Phyllis has been a great testament to the power of faith and perseverance. Faith test and tried, but victory on the other side.

AUDRA WILSON
The Pregnancy Resource Center, Keene, New Hampshire

I am reminded that when a woman is pregnant with a girl, she actually is carrying her grandchild in her womb as well! A baby girl still in the womb has all the eggs in her ovaries prior to being born that she will have as a mature adult woman. Therefore, the birth mother is carrying her grandchildren in her womb too! Awesome! The same understanding came to me for the House of Hope NH! As women come into the House of Hope NH, they will come with future dreams and future visions for themselves they, at the present time, are not even aware of. House of Hope NH will have, contained in her womb, these women who within themselves will have God's gifts and callings these women are not even aware of. These gifts and callings WILL give birth to ministries empowered by the Lord, Yes, House of Hope NH is far bigger than any of us realize.

PASTOR MATTHEW WORRALL
Grace Christian Fellowship, Winchester, New Hampshire

If staying faithful to God through severe trials has always baffled you, this book is the key to unlocking that mystery. A powerful testimony about the love, grace, mercy, and patience of God, it will undoubtedly cause you to stop and reflect on the power of faith in a life willing to trust Jesus through it all. From tragedy to triumph, this uplifting story testifies that only God can take a sinful and rebellious life, and by His Spirit, make it a blessing to humanity. In my 48 years of preaching, this is one book I can recommend to prove Jesus will never leave us nor forsake us.

PASTOR ROBIN DUQUETTE
New Life Chapel, Spofford, New Hampshire

My mother's story is a powerful example of a life turned around and led by faith. After surviving an incredibly difficult childhood and recovering from addiction, her life didn't suddenly become easy. I witnessed her continually lean on God and watched her faith bring her through each new chapter, no matter how impossible it seemed at the time. This is a powerful story of her continued and persistent trust in God's plan.

RACHEL PAGE
McKinney, Texas

Phyllis Phelps led me to Jesus Christ, and over the years has pointed countless people to Him as well. She has exhibited to me what a Woman of God is. The faith in Christ that Phyllis exudes is amazing, and everything she does points to Him. I am honored and privileged to know her.

SARIAH LANAE HASTINGS
House of Hope NH, Keene, New Hampshire

WEATHERING THE STORM

BREAKING THROUGH THE TEMPEST OF PAIN WITH GOD'S ANCHOR OF HOPE

PHYLLIS PHELPS

Weathering the Storm
by Phyllis Phelps

© 2020 by Phyllis Phelps
All rights reserved.

Edited by Dave Ficere with Patt Ficere and Adam Colwell
Cover Design by Jaime Anaya
Back Cover Photo by Lauren Simeon Photography, Winchester, NH
Typesetting by Katherine Lloyd, THE DESK

Published by Adam Colwell's WriteWorks, LLC through Kindle Direct
Publishing

Printed in the United States of America

Print: ISBN: 978-1-7339956-8-9
eBook ISBN: 978-1-7339956-9-6

All Bible quotations are taken from the KING JAMES VERSION, public
domain.

To my family

To my children: Rachel, my oldest. It was you who caused me to realize how much I needed Christ's redeeming love. You continue to smile through your own trials and twists of life. I'm thankful to have been able to raise you through some of our tough circumstances.

To my son, Matthew: You have become a wonderful provider for your family and a hard worker. We are blessed to have you and your family as a part of ours.

To my daughter, Vanessa, who brings much joy to in the face of adversity. You encourage me with your steadfastness.

My hope is that this book inspires my children to keep walking with the Lord despite life's difficulties. Through all the trials and challenges I write about in this book, I truly have learned to trust in Jesus. May you always do the same and trust Him and Him alone throughout your lives. I thank them for all the meaning and many memories of being their mom. They all pulled together and helped Bill and me when life was at its worse. Their love is so precious to me.

Finally, to my husband, Bill, the man who shares life with me, whether near or far away. We've been side by side through thick and thin as you healed from your accident and many surgeries.

Contents

Acknowledgments

$\mathcal{F}$irst and foremost, I want to acknowledge my Living Hope, Jesus Christ, for paying for my sins with His precious blood, transforming me and delivering me from the power of darkness.

Throughout my life, I have been thankful for those who pointed me to Christ and could see right through my rebellion, anger, and pain. I would like to acknowledge Pastor George Rosado and his wife, Grace, for always being truthful and standing on God's Word. I want to recognize Pastor Robin Duquette and his wife, Barbara, who first shared God's love with me and continued to pray and encourage me to stay the course.

I am grateful to Pastor David Berman and his wife, Brenda, for walking with Bill and me through very painful as well as victorious times. I am also appreciative of Pastor Dave for being an example of a godly man, speaking the truth, and teaching me to trust people again. I am grateful that he loves me when I am a liability, and when I am an asset. I also appreciate that he works so closely with the ladies at House of Hope NH to get to their core issues.

Thank you to Pastor Matthew Worrall for believing from the beginning in what the Lord was doing at House of Hope NH and encouraging me with the Word and prayer when I was so discouraged.

I am thankful to the Body of Christ. I have met so many wonderful people of God all over the country that are part of God's beautiful family.

I want to recognize Dave Ficere, who helped put the words of my story together and make sense of it. He gently worked with me, not realizing how healing it was to tell my testimony in its entirety. He was able to tell by my voice when the pain was overwhelming, and I needed a break.

Also, thanks to Dave's wife, Patt, for her assistance in editing the manuscript. I feel like we have a bond of sisterhood together, and I am thankful for her keen editor's eye and for encouraging me. More than writing a book, this has been a wonderful experience, once again demonstrating that nothing is impossible with God. (Luke 1:37)

I want to acknowledge Adam Colwell for publishing *Weathering the Storm* and recognizing that my story was one worth sharing with the world. I appreciate the excitement and confidence he has shown throughout the process and working with us in getting this book published.

Finally, I want to thank and recognize the founding Board of House of Hope NH for. All seven of you have worked with me with God's guidance to make this vision of a home come to pass. I also want to thank the many donors and encouragers along the way for making this dream a reality.

Note from the Author

The events depicted in this book are related to you as I remember them. Other people in my life may have a different recollection. I did my best not to misrepresent any person, event, or organization in any way. In some cases, I chose not to use an individual's full name or real name so as to not put them in jeopardy or harm's way.

Note from the Editor

I first met Phyllis Phelps on LinkedIn, and as I learned more about her, I suggested she had a terrific story to tell. "Have you considered writing a book? I asked. She had been thinking the same thing but was having trouble getting started. As we talked over the next few weeks, it became evident that God was bringing us together to work on this project, which has become a labor of love for both of us.

Phyllis Phelps is a classic example of God using ordinary people for His glory. Within the pages of *Weathering the Storm*, you'll read about her struggles to overcome addiction, homelessness, and low self-esteem. You'll learn how God intervened to mold her into the woman of faith she is today.

It is my sincere hope that you'll enjoy taking this journey with her and that your faith in the mighty God of redemption will be strengthened and renewed.

Dave Ficere
Phoenix, Arizona
May 15, 2020

Chapter 1

THE ACCIDENT

This is so annoying, I thought, as I struggled to hear the caller on the other end of the phone. I was talking with my hair salon, confirming the next day's appointment. I was surprised by how loud the many sirens were that I was hearing outside my Keene, New Hampshire home.

What is going on? I wondered in irritation, as the sirens continued to grow closer. I was in a hurry and afraid of forgetting one of a million things I had to do.

My husband, Bill, and I had just finished meeting and praying with a couple we were tending to as part of our church's marriage ministry. As we were saying goodbye, the phone rang. It was one of the employees from our landscaping business. He had run into a problem at one of the job sites. Something about the paint at an apartment that we were redoing as a side job. Bill had to inspect it and tell them how to proceed. He left immediately for the ten-minute motorcycle ride to check on the problem. As usual, his $200 helmet stayed behind.

It was a beautiful summer day in New Hampshire. We were busy getting ready for a much-needed vacation, excited to leave for our yearly family getaway. Bill and I, along with our three children:

19-year-old Vanessa, 26-year-old Rachel, and 22-year-old Matthew, were headed north for two nights at Lake Winnipesaukee. There, we were going to attend the Soulfest Christian Music Festival at the nearby Gunstock Mountain Resort. After that, we planned to spend four days at the Sea Spiral Suites Hotel in Hampton Beach, about 100 miles east of our southern New Hampshire home.

The sirens were getting louder and sounded like they were right outside our door as I hung up the phone. Suddenly, for no reason, fear gripped my heart as I thought of Bill, who never wore his helmet on such quick trips despite my wishing he would do so. I had a bad feeling about the ominous meaning of the sirens, coupled with the fact that Bill was overdue.

I expected him back in ten minutes, but a half-hour later he still hadn't returned or phoned, so I called his cell phone. A familiar voice–but not Bill's–answered. It was our friend, Jazz, who spoke before I could say anything. "Bill has been in a terrible motorcycle accident," she told me. "Serena and I had just walked out of the store and saw it happen. We were on the scene in seconds, well before police and the ambulance arrived. Bill is alive, but not doing well." Jazz told me that her daughter Serena used her nursing skills to help clear Bill's air passageway. If not for the two of them, he would have died at the scene.

I was too stunned to speak and then began getting angry. I was terrified over Bill's fate and that he hadn't worn his helmet. "Oh, God, no!" I finally cried out, falling to my knees. But Jazz stopped me in my tracks. "You need to stop. Your husband needs you. Your family is going to need you. You can't do this. You need to focus." Her words sounded harsh and unfeeling, but I knew they were spoken in love from one Christian sister to another. It was exactly what I needed to hear.

Meanwhile, Matthew ran upstairs from the basement in

response to my cries. "Your dad's been in a bad motorcycle wreck," I whispered to Matthew through my tears. He immediately put his fist through the wall in anger. Matthew hated that his dad rode a bike and had dreamed about this type of accident. As a result, he was terrified of the motorcycle.

That was July 27, 2009, the day my life changed forever, and God began revealing His love to me in a way I could never have imagined. I later learned that the driver of a cable company service truck pulled out in front of Bill at a busy intersection near downtown Keene. Although it's a four-way stop, drivers habitually roll through the red light when turning right, and that's what happened. Even though Bill's bike was bright red and easily visible, the truck driver cut him off, causing Bill to swerve and lose control. He was ejected and flew 40 feet into the air like a rag doll. The accident happened about 1:15 p.m. right before I heard the sirens begin. The truck driver had been on his cellphone and didn't see Bill turning at the light.

Bill's body bounced on the pavement three times, and he banged his head repeatedly. The sirens that had so annoyed me were the first responders speeding to the scene. Bill suffered a traumatic brain injury from hitting the pavement and trying to stand up at least once. He was barely alive.

Immediately after getting off the phone with Jazz, Matthew and I left for the nearby Cheshire Medical Center. Because I was too upset to drive, we hopped into his car, even though it had a broken windshield from him punching it angrily just minutes after he put his fist through the wall. I was quiet and could not stop shaking during the five-minute drive. Matthew, however, vented his anger with a verbal barrage of profanities. I remember crying out in my spirit, asking God and the Holy Spirit to help me. Everything else was just a blur.

I was frantic but with a strange sense of calm as we arrived at the hospital. I spoke with Dr. Tom Provost, a family friend who worked on Bill, and helped prep him for the helicopter ride to a better-equipped medical center. He was one of the first to see Bill in the emergency room and had stayed with him. Dr. Provost came out of the ER to see me in the waiting room.

"Please don't lie to me," I told him. "Tell me how it is."

"Well, we can't help your husband here. We have to fly him out to Dartmouth. You can come back and see him."

The doctors let me into the emergency room cubicle as they were prepping Bill for the flight. The room was cold, sterile, and stark, a somber reminder of the battle for life to all who entered. There weren't any machines monitoring Bill, just several IV bags connected to his arms. When I saw my husband of more than 20 years, he looked like he was dead. He didn't move but was conscious. I felt so helpless and couldn't even speak or hug him. All I could do was cry out to God.

Lord, I just pray for my husband, and I know that the chances are slim, I pleaded silently.

When I touched Bill's foot, I felt the warmth of life. Hope flooded my soul as if the Lord was saying, "I am with you."

They life-flighted Bill to Dartmouth Hitchcock Medical Center in Lebanon, the only Level One trauma center in New Hampshire, and the best hospital in the state. They wouldn't let me fly with him because of the liability, and in case he didn't survive. That meant we had to make a 75-minute trip in the car.

Matthew returned home and swapped his car for mine and brought Vanessa back with him. They couldn't find Rachel, even though she and Vanessa worked in the same building and left her a phone message before heading back to Cheshire.

After Matthew arrived, a pastor friend drove Vanessa and me

to Dartmouth in my car. Matthew and a friend came separately. Little was said during the drive, but we shed many tears and prayed silently. It was one of the longest trips of my life.

Immediately after arriving at Dartmouth, the doctors found us and handed me Bill's wedding ring. They told us to come in and say goodbye and explained the severity of his injuries. The doctors said they had to perform brain surgery immediately if Bill was to survive.

"There's not much hope we can give you," they said, adding that Bill would never walk or talk again or have "normal" functions. He would be a vegetable for the rest of his life.

"He's going to die if we don't give him this operation," the doctors said. "You have three minutes to decide."

"If there's any hope at all," I told them, "give him the operation."

Rachel had gotten the phone message and had to find a sitter for my granddaughter before heading to Dartmouth. She would arrive later, upset that she couldn't be with us at this crucial moment in our family's life.

Vanessa and Matthew were there with me as we went into the room to say goodbye to Bill. The three of us joined hands. I knew the kids were looking to me for leadership and how I would react. I could see it in their eyes, even though they didn't say a word. It was one of those teachable moments parents have with their children. "You know, the doctors don't have the final say," I told the kids through my tears, "but God does, so we're gonna pray."

We prayed. I watched my children with their dad, wondering if that was the last time they'd ever see him alive. So, the three of us joined hands. Everyone was crying as I prayed, "Lord, if he lives, okay. If not, okay, but You have the final say."

Bill was so banged up that none of us wanted to touch his face or arms out of fear that we would do more harm. Silence enveloped the room as no one knew what to say. So, after we prayed, we all touched his leg and quietly left the room.

A team of neurosurgeons went to work. Bill had suffered broken ribs, a punctured lung, crushed bones on his right side, a broken jaw, and fractured bones in his leg and ankle. His brain stem was nearly severed in the wreck, and they rebuilt his skull using five titanium plates. He was placed into the Critical Care Unit, where people were dying around us, and you could feel the grip of death in the air. The doctors told me that had the accident happened one hour later, Bill would have died. He was airlifted on the last life flight of the day due to an incoming storm that shut down all subsequent flights. God was definitely watching over us!

As Bill was wheeled off to surgery, I needed to get away and just talk to the Lord without anyone else around. So, I snuck away into the bathroom, closed and locked the door, got on my knees, and said, "Jesus, I'm not ready to lose my husband yet, but if I do, my life is yours."

I laid down everything about me before the Lord. Bill, our marriage, and our business—our whole lives. Our landscaping business was bringing in about $400,000 a year, and we had a nice six-figure income. But it was all going to end that day. During that time of prayer, the Lord reminded me of where I had come from and been through more than 25 years ago. I got down on the floor that afternoon as Phyllis Phelps and came away a different person.

Bill came through the surgeries, but the doctors reminded me again that evening that he might never walk or talk. They weren't sure how he would come out of such a complicated, delicate brain surgery, and it was touch and go for a week. I took a pastor friend and his wife with me for moral support when they let me in to see him. Bill was hooked up to multiple machines and a breathing tube. The side of his head was an entirely different shape. I sobbed.

For the next week, the doctors came to me every evening and said, "Mrs. Phelps, he's not going to make it through the night." I would stay with Bill and pray over him. I would whisper in his ear, "You shall live and not die." The Lord spoke to me, and I remembered Psalm 23, as I heard the moans of people dying around me. I thought about the sheep and the security they enjoy knowing the shepherd is near. Psalm 23 became real to me, especially verse six:

> Surely goodness and loving kindness will follow me
>   all the days of my life,
> And I will dwell in the house of the LORD forever.

The doctor's words echoed in my ears, but the Lord said to me, "Are you going to believe the report of the Lord or the report of the doctor? Who are you going to believe?"

"Lord, I trust you," I responded.

We are well known in our community, so word about the accident spread quickly. Seven pastors came together at an area church to fast and pray for Bill. Hundreds of people showed up at Dartmouth and waited in the hallways, praying for us as well. Some were friends or people we knew from various churches or business connections. Others were perfect strangers who felt the need to be there for us. Our church home group showed up and prayed for us in the waiting room. While I appreciated all the love and prayers from everyone, I honestly didn't want people around. Strangely, I felt that I had to entertain them when, in reality, I just wanted to fade into the woodwork. I was numb and didn't want to talk to anyone.

We were also badgered by the media. The local newspaper

wrote several stories about the accident before even talking to me. At one point, there were more than 100 phone messages on my answering machine from media outlets.

The hospital staff noticed all of the people showing up and the attention we were getting. While they typically don't like extra people hanging around, they realized there was something different about them. The Dartmouth staff saw that this group of friends, members of our church family, and others who only knew us by name had faith and hope for Bill's recovery. These visitation angels showered my family and me with affection. Some visitors brought us food and prayed with us and others who were facing similar circumstances. The love these friends had for us served as quite a testimony to those working at the hospital.

The hospital staff was wonderful toward us and me in particular. They would save special food for me in the kitchen at the end of the night and noticed when I was in the waiting room praying with others whose loved ones had also been in an accident. We learned that the hospital staff called 2009 "The Summer of Death" because there had been so many motorcycle fatalities. We met and prayed with some of those families during Bill's hospital stay.

One nurse, in particular, saw me praying over Bill as she made her rounds and checked his vital signs. She told me she had seen the difference in me and those who were visiting. "I've been praying for you all night," she told me. God had sent that nurse to minister to me as His angel as I prayed for and stayed with Bill. In every way I can think of, the staff was so full of love, rooting for Bill and encouraging us. They knew—and many believed–that prayer made a difference in Bill surviving the accident and multiple operations for his various injuries. The prayers and caring from others were just two of the many miracles I would experience in the days to come.

Chapter 2

REHAB AND RECOVERY

I stayed day and night at the hospital for the first week but did book a room at a nearby, cheap hotel. It was not a place I would have normally picked, but it was all that was available. Matthew and his wife, Lateesha, stayed there and tried to get me to leave the hospital, but I couldn't. I did give in by staying at the hotel one night for about five hours. Other than that, I was at the hospital around the clock.

Sleep eluded me. In fact, I didn't sleep for the first three days Bill was in the hospital. Even though he had been put into a medically-induced coma the first night at Dartmouth in Lebanon, New Hampshire to slow his brain down and promote greater healing. I would just hug my Bible and pray and only fell asleep after collapsing from exhaustion. During that time, the Lord gave me a verse from Nahum 1:7 to comfort me:

> The Lord is good, a strong hold in the day of trouble;
> and he knoweth them that trust in him.

Despite the doctor's dire predictions, Bill did survive that first week, but he looked very fragile and still wasn't out of the woods. The doctors wanted to see milestones in his recovery, such as the ability to breathe on his own. So, they tried removing his breathing tube but had to reinsert it because his body wasn't ready to breathe on its own yet. He had a tube inserted in the top of his head, draining fluid from his brain and could only get nourishment via a feeding tube. He was also hooked up to several IVs and had an internal tube pushed down toward his heart to monitor a collapsed lung.

The doctors considered breathing on his own a huge first step in Bill's recovery. It happened one day after we returned from lunch at Applebee's near the end of Bill's second week of recovery. While Vanessa and I were out, the doctors removed the breathing tube and waited for us to return. When we did, they didn't say a word, waiting for us to notice. Vanessa saw it first. "Oh, look, mom," she exclaimed, starting to cry and covering her face. That got my attention, and I looked, seeing the same thing she did. Bill was out of the induced coma and breathing independently. We both immediately began crying. Bill couldn't talk and could barely open his eyes, but could blink to acknowledge something we said or asked. When he did so, we again began weeping.

About four hours after the feeding tube was removed, Bill was able to speak, but even then, his speech was only a strained whisper. He could only talk in a low volume and for short bursts, but it was a start. While he could not construct a coherent sentence, remarkably, he could quote Psalm 1. God had preserved that scripture in his damaged brain. Rachel always said, "I love you, dad," when we left, and he would whisper back, "I love you, too." While it marked another step forward, we were beginning to see the outward manifestations of the brain damage caused by the accident. For one thing, Bill didn't recognize us as his family.

Bill continued to make progress and was eventually moved from Critical Care to Intensive Care. After he was taken off the feeding tube, doctors began gradually introducing solid food into his diet and "thickened" water. This process involved putting a teaspoon of solid material into his water to slow down the drinking process. Bill had to relearn how to eat and drink all over again, and they put him in a protective tent to minimize the impact of germs. Bill would touch my ring and fingers because he was discovering textures as if for the first time.

At the same time, Bill was on a lot of drugs, and some of them caused hallucinations. He wanted out of the hospital and couldn't understand why he was there, so sometimes the staff had to tie his hands to the bed so he wouldn't rip the IV lines or tubes out or try to get up and walk. It was painful for me to watch all of this.

We never really talked about the accident or told Bill all of what we knew. The entire accident was a blank in his mind. He couldn't remember the moments before his motorcycle swerved to avoid the truck and he was thrown off his bike. Every morning, I would have to remind him why he was in the hospital and that he had had a motorcycle accident.

Bill was confused and scared most of the time. He didn't know who we were or where home was. We threw him a fortieth birthday party the February before the accident, but he didn't remember any of it. I remembered the doctors telling me that Bill would suffer memory loss because the damage occurred in the portions of his brain that had experienced the bleeding. This accounted for some of his memory issues and the loss of cognitive functions. Some memories are gone forever, while others come back inaccurately or with just partial recall.

Doctors had wanted me to consider institutionalizing Bill,

but I didn't even want to entertain that thought. My children and I never discussed the option while Bill was hospitalized, and it never came up until much later on in our lives. I think our children would have been more objective about that option than I was. Especially considering the long road to recovery ahead between the hospital, the rehabilitation center, and eventually going home.

When you go through something as traumatic as I did, it's both easy and natural to focus on the event at hand and let other things lapse. Such was the case for me, which became evident when I went to pay for my hotel room and found that the IRS had frozen the debit card linked to our business checking account. The card worked at the hotel without a problem when I checked in. I can only assume it must have been frozen during that week at the hospital. Even though we had about $30,000 in the account, the IRS froze it due to non-payment. We were on a payment plan to catch up on overdue back taxes and had missed quarterly payment. I must have also not seen the warning letters they sent because I was dealing with the aftermath of Bill's accident. Even so, it was unusual for the IRS to act so quickly. My church stepped in and paid the one-week hotel room bill of about $850 while I made a mental note to contact the IRS to get our accounts straightened out.

During Bill's two-week hospital stay in Manchester, I would return home on Fridays to take care of our seven-employee business payroll. My niece helped out during the week with the billing and day-to-day details of running a business, and that was a huge help to me. Not only was the Lord carrying us, but he also used many people who came along at the right time with just what we needed to take the next step. As for the IRS, we went back and forth over the phone for several weeks, but the missed payment situation got resolved in the next few months. They unfroze our checking account, and we were able to get back on track.

While at Dartmouth, Bill began intensive rehab and was transferred from there in August to Catholic Medical Center (CMC) in Manchester. Finding CMC was an answer to prayer. Rachel and I spent a lot of time looking for a rehab facility. We were appalled at what was out there. Many of the facilities were depressing, smelled like urine, and felt like a nursing home. We cried, desperate to find the right place for Bill, and I prayed, "Lord, I really need to know where to send him." We had to find something by August 10, which was the date the insurance company had set for Bill to leave Dartmouth. While we were driving around, I saw a huge banner that said, "Construction starting August 10." That banner was right in front of the exit to CMC, and I knew God was guiding us there.

CMC is the top heart hospital in the area, and the home of the nationally-renowned New England Heart & Vascular Institute. It is rated among the top cardiovascular programs in the country and God's guidance was reaffirmed when Bill started developing blood clots. This development led to more surgeries, and we couldn't have received better care than we did at CMC.

One funny memory I have from Bill's stay at CMC was pushing him in a wheelchair on a skywalk connecting two of the buildings. I temporarily lost control, and the wheelchair nearly got away from me. I could just picture Bill's chair rolling out of control down the skywalk with me chasing it. Today, we can laugh about it, but at the time it was pretty scary.

Bill stayed at Catholic Medical Center until September, about six weeks after first arriving. Every single day was a struggle as he had to relearn life's basic skills all over again. We had to teach him how to eat and how to walk and talk. It was difficult for him to accept, and he fought it. It was hard for me to watch, but I knew that the Lord was still in control. Rehab continued after Bill returned home, but he kept resisting. Because it was so painful, he eventually stopped going to rehab and speech therapy. He quit doing his stretches and receiving occupational therapy. He was non-compliant and didn't understand why people were asking him to do things and frustrated that he couldn't do what they asked him to. He lashed out at me over what they were asking him to do and eventually just gave up.

"I can't find myself," he said to me one day. He was also angry that he was alive and begged me to shoot him. "Why didn't you let me die?" he asked me angrily one day.

☙

Our children were waiting at home on September 10, 2009, the day their dad came home from the hospital. Bill was scared to return home, angry, and frustrated that he couldn't function as he used to and confused about what was now his new reality. When we got home, he didn't recognize it as his house. He couldn't remember the names of some people and how he knew them. "I can't find myself. I feel so lost," he told me.

Bill often had a blank look in his eyes like someone in a drug-induced fog. At times he had difficulty communicating with me and the kids. At the same time, he was prone to angry outbursts and was demanding of me. When he wanted something, he wanted it now. The children also experienced this intense anger and did not see many expressions of love from him. For them, it was as if a different person masquerading as Bill had come home from the hospital. This person was not the "dad" they knew.

As a result, what should have been a joyous and happy homecoming was fraught with anger, struggle, tension, and anxiety for our entire family. It affected everyone, but the emotional turmoil of Bill's return hit me the hardest since I was around all the time. I tried to do it all and keep everything together for my family.

Three days after Bill came home, Pastor David Berman from the Christian Life Fellowship Church in Swanzey, New Hampshire, came to visit us. He prayed and anointed Bill with oil, and the Lord gave him Matthew 6 to share with us. "You've built your house on the rock," he said, reminding us that Jesus was with us and would not forsake us during this time of need. He was always there when we called and encouraged me to stay in fellowship with others in our church family and to not be afraid to ask for help.

Bill's homecoming began three years of intense struggle, new challenges, and a lot of emotional pain for our family. There were times, I have to confess, that I would give him medicine just to get him to calm down and stop his ranting and raving. The kids all reacted differently to Bill. Rachel, married and out of the house, was more patient and understanding. Vanessa began reading a book about brain injuries we had been given. She stayed positive, prayed, and kept her hopes alive for a miracle. As a result, she got along with Bill better than anyone else in the family. Matthew continued to be very angry because he lost his best friend and didn't like the way Bill treated me.

It hurt me to see Matthew this way. In reality, having Bill home was like having another child but in a man's body. I had no idea that when I gave the okay for his operation, this would be the result. I've often struggled with the question, "Did I make the right decision?" Even years later, the kids still struggle with the aftermath of the accident. They grieve over who their dad is now compared to how they remember him before the crash.

Once, while riding in our truck, Bill couldn't remember the roads. Crying, he turned to me and said, "My life now is like having a favorite book and opening it every day to read. Then one morning, I opened it, and all the beautiful words were gone. The pages were empty." He was trying to explain how he felt in a way I could understand since he knew that I love to read. "Bill," I replied, "we'll just rewrite that book together."

During Bill's initial recovery, we experienced painful moments almost every day, and I made a lot of mistakes. Most of those errors were financial and having to do with our business. I made mistakes like putting someone in charge who wasn't capable of handling things or trying to keep the business going by myself, juggling everything at once, and refusing to let some things go. No one from our church or from the business community offered to help us with the business, probably because they knew I wouldn't be able to turn it over to them.

I also wrestled with decisions such as whether or not to buy a car. I was afraid of making yet another mistake. It was at that point, in the midst of it all, that my sister Roberta looked at me and said, "You know what, Phyllis? Just make the mistakes. It's okay." I bought the car and didn't look back.

In the next two years, through all the surgeries, more than 200 doctors would work with Bill, and he ended up with five titanium plates in his head holding his skull together. The doctors warned us that it might set off the airport metal detectors when we traveled (it did), but it is just one more opportunity to trust God.

BEGINNINGS

I was born in 1964, the last year of the Baby Boomer generation. The average home cost about $13,000, gasoline was 30 cents a gallon, and a loaf of bread cost only 21 cents. The Beatles held the top five positions on the Billboard Top 40 singles chart, and race riots broke out in several U.S. cities. Overseas, American soldiers were dying in the killing fields of Southeast Asia as the Vietnam War was ramping up.

My mom, Joyce, had her first out-of-wedlock child at the age of 16. She had two more children by the time she was 23 when I came along. I was the fourth of five children in our family and the third girl. Life was tough for my mom. She was an unwed mother forced to run away from home because my grandmother had threatened to abort my oldest sister with a coat hanger. Dad frequently gambled away his paycheck, drank a lot, and was a member of a motorcycle "club," which, in reality, was a biker gang. I didn't realize it then, but today I know he also had a gambling addiction.

My dad never married my mom and lived only for himself. He left us when I was 10 months old and never returned. Because there was little money, we were hungry most of the time and lived in a tiny shack on California Street in Swanzey, New Hampshire. Mom would walk five miles to the Swanzey Woolen Mill, work the night shift, and walk back home late at night.

When I was two, my mom met and married my stepfather, and that led to years of molestation and abuse at his hands. He and my mom fought all the time verbally and physically. It sometimes went on late into the night and was bloody and horrible. There were whips and guns involved, and I remember someone's head going through a window during one such altercation. Amazingly, no one was shot and killed during these scuffles. I was afraid most of the time and would hide in a tree when my stepfather called my name because I was scared of what he would do. He did cruel things to torture me, killing my pet cats and leaving them on the doorstep. It was horrible! I lived in a survival mode, and the only time I felt safe was at school. I was even fearful about staying home from school when I was sick, terrified over what he would do to me on his lunch break from work. We weren't allowed to cry—that only made things worse—and couldn't tell anyone the truth about what was happening in our home. I thought everyone lived like we did because no one talked about what was actually going on. In reality, other girls faced the same abuse I did. However, nobody talked about it within or outside of the family.

I remember another trauma during that same period in my life. One time, we were visiting my uncle's house when someone backed over me with a car. I ended up in the hospital with leg and back injuries. The doctors put me into an induced coma, where I stayed for about two weeks. But God was there protecting me, even though I didn't see it at the time.

When I was about five, my mom found out about the molestation. It changed her and not in a positive way. She began drinking, doing drugs, and abusing prescription medications. It was her way of dealing with the pain in her life. One time she overdosed, convulsing on the floor. All I could think of as my sisters tried to help her was that I wanted her to live, so we wouldn't be left living with this monster of a stepfather. *What's gonna happen is we're going to be lost to this guy*, I thought. Later in life, people would tell me they were surprised I survived my family situation.

We didn't go to church, so I did not receive any religious instruction. One older neighbor, Mrs. Guion, was very motherly and would occasionally take of us neighborhood kids to Sunday School. Still, none of it made an impression on me. I remember her taking us to the local Church of God, where they didn't use any musical instruments but sang everything acapella. I thought about God but wondered if He even existed. I remember asking Him once in prayer, "Why did you create me to be abused? You created me for pain." I hated Him because He was supposed to be my Creator, but left me in this dark, dark place that I couldn't escape from.

I didn't want to go down the same path as my mom, but at the age of 10, I started drinking before school. Up until that point, I got pretty good grades, but by the seventh grade, I was on a downward spiral. By the time I was 12, I was experimenting with drugs and was uncontrollable. My grades went from "A's" to "F's," and my mom couldn't figure out what was going on. I would leave for days at a time and eventually get picked up by the police. They never charged me with a crime but would threaten to send me to juvenile hall if I kept running away. Once I tried to run from them, and my parents had to pick me up at the police station after I was there for four hours. I was so full of pain from the abuse and my unstable home life that no drugs could deaden the hurt. The downward spiral of anger, hurt, and drugs kept moving faster, but I couldn't get high enough to numb the pain. Instead of closing the hole in my life, drugs and alcohol only made it larger.

I was about 12 when I saw a man preaching from the Bible on the corner at the Commons in nearby Keene. He told me, "Jesus loves you." I just lost it. I screamed at him. "I hate you, and I hate your God! He's not my God! He created me for pain." I ranted, swearing at him profusely. He just put his Bible down, bowed his head, and walked away. I think he was praying for me, but I remember that when he told me that Jesus loves me, I felt a searing pain as if someone was pouring hot coffee all over my body. The light of God's Word and love hit the darkness of my life, and I couldn't stand it. I was full of anger and hate, and I was offended by the preacher's words.

On another occasion, someone gave me a Gideon Bible, which I put under my pillow. I held onto it for protection when my stepfather came into my room, holding a whip and machete. I was frightened. I clutched the Bible, thinking it had some mystical power, and prayed. "Lord, if you're real and save me tonight, then I promise I'll serve you." Of course, I did not keep that promise then, but I can now see that there were little glimpses of God along the way as I struggled through adolescence.

My mom had it pretty rough with me because I was a tough kid who would hang out with my friends on Main Street. I grew to hate her because I felt that she could have done a better job protecting me from her boyfriends and my stepfather. She just refused to stand up for herself or us kids, and I resented her for it. I remember times when there wasn't any food in the refrigerator, but there was plenty of beer. I hated living this way.

One Christmas Eve, my stepfather held a gun to my sister's

head and threatened to kill us. He had been drinking, and although he and my mom had separated, he came back to the house armed and in a drunken rage. We called the police, and he was arrested, but they warned us he would be released from jail in four hours. So, we quickly moved out because mom was afraid that he would come back and follow through on his threat. Mom wanted to keep all of us kids together because my stepfather was well known and respected in the community. She didn't know who she could trust if she farmed us out to stay with others. So, six of us (including my half-brother) ended up living in a camper in a freezing field with only a small heater to keep us warm. You can imagine living in cramped quarters during a New Hampshire winter, where the average high is about 34 with temperatures dipping into the teens at night. It was quite crowded for us, but at least my stepfather didn't know where we were. A short time later, my mom insisted that my 14-year-old pregnant sister move in with her boyfriend so that we would have more room.

About four months later, we moved out of the camper and in with one of my mom's friends into what I called the "party" house. Although it was warmer during the cold of winter, in some ways, it was a worse environment. For one thing, there were always parties happening and a lot of noise. People came and went at all hours of the day and night and trashed the house. Once I had to clean up all the vomit everywhere from revelers throwing up. People would pass out, and we'd have to step over them to leave for school. My sisters and I often huddled together in the bedroom with the door locked, while mom participated in the partying because we didn't trust the men who were in the house. I slept with a knife under my mattress and probably would have traded it for a gun if I had had access to one. We lived in constant fear and turmoil, and it got to the point where my sisters and I realized no one was going to protect us, and we had to defend ourselves.

Throughout this time, I was angry and bitter, and my heart turned black. I gained a lot of strength from the hatred and anger that kept me going and blocked out other emotions. Back then, I thought these emotions were making me stronger, but now I see they were holding me captive and binding me.

My only desire was to kill my stepfather for the pain and suffering he had caused me and my family. My sisters and I talked about our situation, but I never let them know what I was thinking. I schemed about how to do away with him, and if I could have gotten ahold of a gun, I probably would have shot him. The following February, he was home alone at the house–where we still had some of our stuff—when it caught fire. We lost everything, and my stepfather died in the blaze. I'm convinced that had he not died in the fire, I would have eventually—except for God's intervention—killed him and now be in jail for murder. The only way I would have escaped prison was by pleading self-defense.

After the fire, we moved in with another one of mom's friends from work in one of the many moves we made that year. It was a much more secure location and a stable environment. We had supper at the table every night, and I had a bedtime, something which was foreign to me because I always did what I wanted. There were also other rules to follow, such as doing chores and speaking respectfully to others. There was no swearing or smoking allowed in the house, and none of us liked the new restrictions. I remember my mom and sisters arguing with the lady of the house over doing the dishes. As a result, we didn't live there long and moved again. Mom had a lot of different boyfriends during this time in my life, and every time she changed boyfriends or had a disagreement, we had to move. This was the pattern for about two years, us hopping around from one place to another.

Amazingly, through all the moves, I was able to stay in the same high school, but my behavior went from bad to worse. I quickly found the other "stoners" in school and started hanging out with them, living to get high, and taking anything I could get my hands on. "Speed," the street term for amphetamines, was popular and thought of as the "poor man's cocaine." I was stoned every available minute, and when I wasn't high, I was miserable. I schemed about how I could get drugs the next day and thought about it all the time. I would steal things from my mom and sisters to the point where they had to lock everything up. My lunch money was spent on drugs, even if that meant going hungry. I even got stoned with my mom once, smoking marijuana with her. Mom was also hooked on prescription drugs and couldn't even get out of bed some days because she was so out of it.

I still remember that on my fourteenth birthday, she was so wasted that I didn't get a birthday card, cake, party, or gifts. I felt like my birthday was meaningless. There was rarely food in the refrigerator, and once I got violently ill after eating a rotten salad that had been in there for a long time. But I was so hungry, I took a chance and paid the price. I was also having a really tough time with my family. I remember one occasion riding in the car after my mom picked me up from babysitting a few kids for her friends. I was so depressed and told her, "I wish I was dead." My mom was so angry that she responded, "Well, I wish you had never been born." It cut me deeply, through every layer of my heart, and just reiterated my hatred for her, further widening the wedge between us.

While Mom was okay with me smoking marijuana, she soon realized I was into heavier stuff and became concerned. One night I came home really messed up, and she was going to take me to the hospital. "She's doing drugs, mom," my sister told her, talking her out of taking me to the hospital. I was also hanging out with some dangerous people. Once they called and threatened to take me from her, telling my mom I wasn't coming home from school and that I "belonged to them now." It really scared her, and after their threats, I did my best to keep them away, and they never threatened her again. I was so naïve, thinking they were just people to hang out and get high with. In reality, some of them were drug dealers and members of either the Westport Boys or Troy Boys gangs. The Troy Boys were notorious bullies who terrorized the nearby town of Troy in the 1970s. One time, they dragged a man who owed them money behind a truck, killing him. Eventually, five of the Troy Boys were convicted of multiple murders and sent to prison. Although I never witnessed any of their behavior, I quickly learned to avoid them.

Some days, instead of taking us to school, the bus driver would drop several of us off at the drug house where the gang members hung out. This particular driver would take us anywhere we wanted to go. I would go to the drug house instead of school two or three times in a typical week. Eventually, I got caught ditching school by the truant officer, who called my mom. That was the end of the drug house visits.

While Mom never tried to get me into drug rehab, one of my sisters offered me money to stop, but I didn't take her up on her offer. A turning point for my mom was seeing a bag of marijuana on the table next to my bed and realizing how badly messed up I was. Even though she was going through her own struggles and didn't have a relationship with God, she realized I was getting in deep and needed help. She slowly began turning to God because our family circumstances were desperate. Mom began praying for me, realizing how dangerous my situation had become. She later told me she remembered asking God, "Could you please get my daughter out of this?"

About the same time, my oldest sister came to Christ through a friend who invited her to church. She brought home some Scripture tracts for me to read. I didn't get the words but was struck by the picture. It showed a chasm. A man on a cliff was on one side with Christ on the other. A cross formed a bridge over the divide. My sister was constantly pestering me to go to church with her. One night I said to the Lord, "I will go to church in the morning, but you better show up if you're real, or else I'll never set foot in a church again." So, I went with her and accepted Christ there, going forward during the invitation. I didn't understand anything. I remember being scared to go to the front of the church during the altar call. Suddenly, a lady sitting behind me tapped me on the shoulder and asked me if I wanted to go forward. I nodded, and she helped me make it up to the front of the church. When I got there, I knelt down to pray and saw a man with a white robe and sandals running toward me when I asked Christ to forgive me of my sins and come into my life. It felt like darkness was leaving me. It was physically painful because I had so much going on in my life and so much pain.

Despite my dramatic conversion, I didn't break away from the drug lifestyle. However, I did read the Bible for three straight days and nights without even taking a break to eat. I wanted to know this God I had accepted into my heart. However, I didn't understand the lifestyle change that needed to accompany my faith. In my new found self-righteousness, I told my mom she was miserable and going to Hell. When I said this, she thought I was in a cult and decided to check it out. She did and accepted Christ into her heart. I told God I didn't want her to come to Christ because I didn't love my mother. While I should have been overjoyed at her new expression of faith, I was quite upset.

Chapter 4

STRUGGLING AT HOME

Mom changed radically after coming to Christ. She quit drugs and stopped smoking almost immediately while I continued grappling with the same issues. *It just isn't fair that mom is free from all this, while I'm still struggling*, I thought. She was living with her boyfriend at the time, but the Holy Spirit so convicted her that she eventually married him and began laying down rules I had to abide by.

I think all the changes in my mom, and those she implemented at home, fueled more rebellion and resentment. It also slowed my response to the things of God. Somehow, I felt that He loved her more than He loved me. The abuse I had suffered at the hands of my stepfather, coupled with the poor example from my biological father, warped my image of God as a loving Father.

I was being pulled in two directions because I still enjoyed my sin but was now uncomfortable participating in it. It was the classic dilemma Paul referred to in Romans and Galatians as the battle between the Spirit and the flesh. My life was Ground Zero for this battle, and I was miserable. My only sign of spiritual growth involved swearing. I remember thinking one day, *Wow, I haven't sworn for a while.* That was radically different from my family environment, and my personal language, which was colorfully and liberally sprinkled with choice swear words.

Our church organist, Eleanor, tried her best to follow up and disciple me in the things of God. She was on fire for the Lord and would come to visit, feeding me God's Word and challenging me to live for Christ. But I was still rebellious and was dealing with so many other issues. My resentment toward both my mom and stepfather hampered any efforts others made to help me grow in Christ. Eleanor, along with the pastor's wife, Barbara, and others all tried to help me spiritually, but I didn't accept it. I was still clinging to bitterness and had not forgiven my mom or stepfather for their behavior toward me. Spiritually, it was one step forward and one backward.

Mom's new rules included being home by a particular time, changing who I was hanging out with, and eating dinner at the table. These, coupled with her changed life, just led to more rebellion on my part, and our home became a battleground. I opposed her at every turn, fighting against it all, and finally left home so I could be free of the rules and restrictions. My mom was planning a special event for my sixteenth birthday, possibly to make up for my fourteenth birthday non-event, but I skipped it and left to move in with my boyfriend. I had had enough of the rules! "Don't you know that I love you?" my mom asked one day in another of her constant efforts to reach out to me. *Too little, too late,* I thought. *My life is ruined!*

Even though my mom had come to Christ, she was very broken and carried a lot of guilt. I'm sure she blamed herself for my lifestyle and the problems I was having because of the bad example she had set. All during the next year, my mom would try to talk me into coming back home and returning to church. Still, I wouldn't listen and continued living my life of partying, drinking, and doing drugs. I didn't completely walk away from God but wasn't living for Him, continuing to live in rebellion.

Meanwhile, my boyfriend wasn't working so I had to get a job working overnights, from 11:00 p.m. until 7:00 a.m. Coworkers gave me some white pills to help me stay awake, and then a strange thing happened. The drugs and drinking started making me violently ill, and I wound up quitting my job because I was sick all the time.

On my eighteenth birthday, I was shocked to learn that I was three months pregnant. The illness I was experiencing was pregnancy-related and not a result of substance abuse. I was scared to death. *I'm not taking care of myself; how can I take care of a baby?* I wondered. I told my boyfriend, and he said he wanted to marry me, but I didn't want to marry him because I saw no future for us.

"There are other options, you know," the doctor told me. Knowing that he was talking about abortion, I looked at him and replied, "That's not an option for me." It was ingrained in me that abortion was wrong, so I never considered it for even a second. But I also quickly realized that I needed to get out of the unhealthy relationship with my unemployed boyfriend because of his lifestyle and the fact that he liked running around with other women.

I think everyone in my family always assumed that I would have and keep the baby because they knew I opposed abortion. So, broke, pregnant, and still battling sickness, I moved back home. With the illness and my pregnancy, I couldn't work. Some days I was so sick that I couldn't even lift my head off of the pillow. I was so dysfunctional that I think most of my family members assumed that one of them would help raise my baby. But I never entertained the option of having someone else raise my child.

Having to move back home with my tail between my legs, so to speak, was embarrassing and a reality check for me. It sobered me up temporarily, and I immediately stopped doing drugs and drinking while trying to reestablish my relationship with God. It was hard because I was so messed up and wasn't getting much support at home. The church had few resources for someone like me, and those who tried to help didn't know what to do with me. I felt like such a burden on my family, but I had nowhere else to go. I wanted to change my ways, and, in that sense, moving back home was a blessing because I was out of the toxic environment I had with my boyfriend. Because I was so sick, depressed, and carrying a child, my mom and family tried to nurse me back to health. It should have been a good thing for me because my mom was remarried and dealing with her issues. But my new stepfather was strict, and I hated all his restrictions. Because he was now a Christian, he wanted to be the head of the household and imposed some reasonable rules. But they weren't "reasonable" to me, so I continued rebelling against his authority.

Ironically, I had known my new stepfather before he and my mom got together. We were even friends; that is, until he married my mom. Although he never had children of his own, he tried his best to be a dad to me, but it was difficult for him. I'm sure at times he asked himself, "What have I gotten myself into?" He had come to the Lord out of the trucking lifestyle and changed his ways, too. While it was a good thing that both he and my mom were now believers, he expected me to respect and follow their new rules, but I didn't want to. So, I bounced between my oldest sister's house and my mom's when things got rough at home. Despite being a "new Christian" family, ours was still quite dysfunctional! I wasn't thankful to be home, didn't want to be home, and didn't want to be pregnant. I felt that my life was a bad dream. My depression worsened throughout the pregnancy, and in March 1983, it was time to have the baby. Because of our strained relationship, my mom dropped me off at the hospital after praying with me and giving me a hug. I went through the birth process alone. I never imagined giving birth would be so painful, and I was scared, confused, and lonely. I remember that half of me was cursing, and the other half was praying. I thought the pain was going to kill me, and I wanted to die. But the Lord reassured me, put His hand on my shoulder, and said, "I'm here." He comforted me throughout the birth process as I felt lost, alone, and worthless. Even the doctor, after my daughter, Rachel, was born, came in to check on me and said, "I'll see you next year." I felt that even he was abandoning me. No one visited me, even the next day, to see the baby because they weren't happy about the situation that I had gotten myself into. My older sister was the lone bright spot, bringing a box of clothes and other things for the baby. She said to me, "I don't care what others think. I'm going to help you celebrate the birth of your daughter."

After Rachel was born, I began being slowly pulled back toward the old lifestyle and starting hanging out with familiar friends. While our family began growing in their faith, I continued to do the same things I had always done. I started living the old lifestyle and hanging out with the same people as before my spiritual conversion.

By the time my daughter was about eight months old, I was fully back into that old lifestyle with my friends. My baby's father offered to marry me, but he didn't treat me well, and I didn't want to marry him. Even though I loved my new baby girl, it was a very lonely time in my life. No one wanted to come over or even give me a baby shower. Unfortunately, during this time, the church looked down on unwed mothers. Judgmental and unloving people had made the entire nine-month pregnancy miserable. "You made your bed, so lie in it," was the prevailing thought about the plight of unwed mothers. Very few churches had the resources or the inclination to help people like me.

I soon stopped bouncing between my sister's and mom's houses to provide some stability for my daughter and me. But being back at my mom's was difficult because I wasn't working, and I knew I was a burden to others. I was enjoying my daughter, but no one wanted to take in an unwed mom and her new baby. My family didn't have any money, and it was hard for them to put food on the table for themselves, let alone for another adult and a baby. I remember using dishcloths for diapers because we had no money. I got depressed easily, and no one was offering to help me. Rachel was my motivation for getting out of the pit of despair I was in, and I knew only God could pull me out.

"Lord, help me," I cried out one day in prayer.

Chapter 5

A NEW START

I had left home at age 16 and moved in with my boyfriend. I returned home a few years later, after I learned I was pregnant. I was feeling very lonely, spiraling down into a deep depression, and often thought about suicide. By the age of 19, I felt worthless and abandoned, having had a daughter out of wedlock with no place to call home. Still abusing drugs and alcohol, I wound up staying at my sister's house for a while. Then it was "couch surfing," going from place to place wherever I could find someone to take me and my baby girl in. I had not genuinely surrendered my life to the Lord, but He had put fear into me about going back to the old life. However, Satan isn't easily discouraged, and the battle within me raged.

I had decided to leave my old friends because I realized they were not a good influence. I didn't want my daughter to be living in and exposed to that environment. These friends eventually thought I had pretty much dropped off the face of the earth, and from their point of view, I had. But soon enough, I found a new group of people at church through a man I met there. He and I went out to dinner, and I was introduced to his friends, who ended up becoming a new group of "bad friends." They drew me in, but I soon learned they were secretive, did a lot of drinking, stole from their parents, and even "named" their weapons. Some of them were probably druggies, but I never knew for sure because I got out of there before finding out. I recognized their bad influence and didn't want to repeat the destructive cycle I had just escaped. I was desperate and asked God, "Please, somehow, can you move? There is no way out of this situation!"

Even though I didn't realize it, God was pursuing me. Help came when a pastor friend, Robin Duquette, invited me to go see David Wilkerson at Manchester Christian Church. Wilkerson was a well-known Christian evangelist best known for his book, "The Cross and the Switchblade." He was also the senior pastor of the non-denominational Times Square Church in New York City and founder of the addiction recovery program, Teen Challenge.

Desperate for answers, I decided to go and take Rachel with me. She stayed in the church nursery during the service. Dr. Wilkerson preached a sermon entitled, "The Hunter from Hell," and it was as if he was talking directly to me. His message was based on Proverbs 6:26, which says, "For by means of a whorish woman a man is brought to a piece of bread: and the adulteress will hunt for the precious life."

Dr. Wilkerson talked about how Satan looks for the precious life and seeks to destroy those who can be used mightily by the Lord. He spoke about those who had fallen in with the wrong crowd and become hooked on drugs. He said even kids who grew up in a church can fall victim to the one who hunts for the precious life.

The devil "seeks those he can devour Wilkerson told the crowd, referencing I Peter 5:8. "Have you ever thought the reason the devil came after you with such ferocity is that he saw something in you and your hunger for God? He (the devil) hunts down those who are the greatest threat to his kingdom and those who can have the greatest impact for Christ. The devil can tempt you and harass you," Wilkerson added, "but he can't have you. God doesn't do anything in vain. The Lord knows what you're going through, and some of you need to come forward tonight and just open up your spirit and hearts to Him because you've never felt worthy or worthy of His love. It's time to receive the love of Christ right now."

I was visibly shaken by David Wilkerson's powerful message, knowing that God was speaking to me. I decided to go forward. I remember thinking to myself, *I weigh 115 pounds, I have an infant child and only the clothes on my back. I don't even know if my last name is my real last name. This is who I am. I'm the person who isn't going to make it. What can your God do for me?* I was feeling guilty and hoping that this decision to turn to God would stick.

I went down to the front of the church during the altar call. Dr. Wilkerson had people up front waiting to pray with those who came forward. I'll never forget that a 12-year-old boy, whom I never saw again or even got his name, prayed powerfully for me. A member of the church's youth group, he began coming against the enemy in prayer and asking God to set me free. It was as if he knew everything I was going through. Even though I had accepted Christ previously, this decision and prayer were powerful, and I felt a special anointing from the Holy Spirit as this boy prayed for me. It felt steady and secure.

After the meeting, Pastor Duquette and I drove back to my mom's house. He was quiet during the return trip because he had watched me make an earlier decision for Christ at his church, but my life had not shown it. He didn't know what I was thinking, and if I was serious about changing this time. *Did she really mean this?* he wondered. We arrived at my mom's house, where we prayed, and he told me about a home for women in need.

New Life Home for Women in Manchester, New Hampshire had been established seven years earlier in 1977 as a place where women could have their lives restored. It is a voluntary, residential treatment facility that serves as a shelter for abused women, helping them get clean from the effects of drugs and alcohol. New Life was an answer to prayer and also had a connection to David Wilkerson. The home's founder, George Rosado, had gone through the Teen Challenge program, become a pastor, and founded New Life because he saw the need for this type of ministry.

"Saving Lives. Empowering Women," was New Life's motto, and it seemed to be a place I could get healthy. I desperately wanted to change but was scared to go there because of their structure and strict rules. It would represent a totally new and foreign environment for me. I was also afraid of failing again, and the people there frightened me. I had learned about the survival of the fittest on the streets. I was wary of others and their motivations.

Pastor Duquette had gone to college with George and said he could help get me into the home. I was invited to go for an interview to see if I would be a good candidate for the New Life program, and I wept during the intake interview. I hadn't cried in a long time, but it felt safe to cry there. My tears were genuine.

"Why do you want to come here and why should we choose you?" the interviewer asked me.

"If you don't choose me, I'm going to die. I have no place else to go."

I was so numb and knew it was either this home or a life of drugs and generational curses. It represented a crossroads for me, and I knew it. I was overcome with emotion and felt a strong presence of the Lord there.

The New Life staff knew I needed more help than the church could give and that I couldn't afford to have someone with me 24/7. It was agreed that I would stay with Eleanor (from my church) for three days to make sure I wasn't doing drugs. I didn't rebel, not wanting to fight anymore because I was scared and emotionally lost. I had no high school diploma and no future. I was so messed up and again cried out to the Lord for help.

There was one hitch, though—New Life didn't accept women with children. But they agreed to make an exception for me because I was adamant that I wouldn't leave my daughter with someone else. I don't know how or why they changed their "no kids" policy to allow me to bring 10-month-old Rachel, as they usually placed children with families in the church. Since then, the home has rebranded itself as Life Home for Women and Children and accepts women who are in the same situation I was.

I remember the ride up to New Life. I knew my family was done with me. My mom, who went with me, said, "This is the last time I'm ever going to help you. If this doesn't work, don't come back." That was hard to hear because I already didn't want to live anymore. Still, I knew it was hard for both my mom and sister to help me financially, especially with a baby. My family, to put it bluntly, was glad to get rid of me. Despite knowing I needed to change, I was scared, nervous, and apprehensive about going to New Life., Yet, I was determined to do anything to change. I wanted to commit my life to Christ and live for Him. But I was confused about how to get from where I was to where I needed to be.

When I showed up at New Life with Rachel, I didn't know

how to receive the love of the Lord even though I had accepted Christ at the David Wilkerson event. Together, the New Life staff taught me about Jesus and how to live for Him, but I had a lot of healing to do. I also had to learn how to work and take care of myself and my daughter.

Arriving at New Life for the first time as a resident, my whole body shook as I walked up the ramp and through the front door. The shaking, I think, represented me leaving my old life and embracing a new one. George and his wife, Grace, took me in as one of their own.

"Welcome home," Grace said, and I immediately felt the love and acceptance from them. I walked upstairs, and she showed me where I would sleep. "This is your bed," she declared. I was overwhelmed by their love, the simple fact of having my own bed, and knowing I didn't have to live in fear. Merely surviving, wondering where I was going to sleep the next night or next month, was a thing of the past. I just had to focus on putting my life back together. I later learned that most of the girls coming to New Life stay anywhere from 18 to 24 months before they're ready to transition back into mainstream society. It takes that long to learn a new way of living and to get clean from drug and alcohol addictions.

Transitioning to New Life was a culture shock, and I was sick for three days. There were two intense weeks of orientation where we had to wear skirts and learn the rules. We were required to ask for everything, even a tissue, because most of us had done everything our own way and on our time schedule for so long that the staff needed to break our old habits. A lot of girls washed out of the program during those first two weeks because it is a grind, especially for "wild" girls who were not used to discipline and structure. As is the case with many recovery programs, I was genuinely learning the concepts of trusting the Lord and living life one day at a time.

After years of poor dietary habits, it was a shock to my system to eat regular, healthy meals, drink a lot of water, and sleep on a normal schedule. Detoxing from unhealthy living made me sick, and I was nervous much of the time. At first, I stayed up a lot at night because I was afraid of the dark, my new surroundings, and those living in the house. But after the rigid daily routine, I was exhausted at the end of the day and ready to sleep. After a while, I got to know and bond with some of the other girls, learning to trust them and realizing they were in the same situation I was. In a short time, they became like family.

The daily routine was rigorous, and there were also seemingly endless Bible studies and devotional times. I rebelled against "all this Bible stuff."

How is this going to change me? I thought. *How is this going to teach me? I need an education. I need a skill. I have nothing. What is this teaching me?*

The Lord had to deal with me about my attitude. It seemed like He was saying, "If you love Me, why is this a burden to you?" I also felt Him saying, "If you want to walk with Me, you need to lay this rebellion down." He was also teaching me the biblical concept of "dying to self," as found in Matthew 16:24-25:

Then said Jesus unto his disciples, If any man will come after me, let him deny himself, and take up his cross, and follow me. For whosoever will save his life shall lose it: and whosoever will lose his life for my sake shall find it.

I needed the routine as a foundation to build on but didn't see it at the time. The daily regimen was almost like that of a military boot camp. We would get up, make our beds, have breakfast, and then devotions using the Our Daily Bread™ booklet. The devotionals included a Scripture passage, an explanation of a biblical principle, and questions to answer. We would record our thoughts in a journal, and the staff would review what we wrote to make sure we were doing the work and sincerely attempting to learn the principles for living.

We were expected to do chores, including extra work for rebelling, not being respectful, or talking back. The staff was good at holding us accountable and showing us tough love when we needed it. They would purposely overcorrect us back into balance since most of the girls (myself included) had come from wild, out-of-control situations. It was a strict environment, and we learned to live in victory and not as victims. "This happened to you, and you have to realize you're not the only one who has been hurt," they told us. We learned to live faithfully for Christ and not look back or wallow in the past.

> And Jesus said unto him, No man, having put his hand to the plough, and looking back, is fit for the kingdom of God. (Luke 9:62)

Putting the hand to the plow symbolized following Jesus, the staff taught us, and once you began plowing, you should not look back. "Are you going to dwell on the negative?" they challenged us. "How are you going to react to the hurt you've experienced? By seeking revenge or exercising forgiveness?"

We also saw that even though people came to New Life from toxic situations, God's love showed through and changed them. The expectations and boundaries were made very clear. Still, it was hard for girls like me that had come out of no-expectation and no-boundary environments. As I said, it was a genuine culture shock!

Although I could leave the home any time I wanted to, I found myself wanting to stay. At first, I thought that all the discipline and rules were part of my being punished. I thought God was chastising me for my past behavior, and the staff members were merely his instruments of punishment. The old thoughts of "being created for pain" crept back into my mind. But the staff helped me deal with that thinking and the resulting self-pity. I came to see them as a blessing and that they did, in fact, care for me. That transformation took about three months as the spiritual principles they taught us began sinking in.

I was learning to embrace the lifestyle change, trust others, and nurture that trust because everyone there was a stranger at first. Part of breaking old patterns meant that none of my friends could write to me, and only five people were allowed to visit. It was hard for me to understand why I was not getting any visitors. Later, I realized that it was a combination of the visitation rules and my family not wanting to come to see me or being able to afford to make the trip.

Not only was I changing and learning new skills, but I also had to take care of Rachel. It was tough taking care of my daughter during this time. But the staff (especially Nellie) helped me a lot, especially when I attended classes. Remember, having an infant at the home was new to them as well, and they were learning how to incorporate that dynamic into their routines. Because of the busy daily schedule, I began feeling that I didn't have enough time with my daughter. So, the staff made adjustments to my routine so I could spend more time with her.

New Life utilized the Teen Challenge curriculum to help us learn new standards and how to develop healthy and

Christian-based values. They focused on character quality, anger management, integrity, relationships, sexual purity, honesty, and thankfulness. Scripture memorization was a large part of the program as well. I also went to a city community education program in Manchester to get my GED. I knew how to read but had to learn how to extract and apply the principles and lessons from what I read. I also learned basic skills, like time management. Different women's groups came in and taught us practical skills such as setting the table and iron clothes. They also ministered to us woman to woman. It was a whirlwind learning experience, and I drank it all in.

The New Life girls, along with George, Grace, and one other staff member, traveled and shared our testimonies and the work of New Life with churches and other Christian organizations. We stayed with families in the towns we passed through and used the trips to raise funds for the home, which functioned as a non-profit ministry. We visited the prominent Brooklyn Tabernacle in New York City and met some wonderful people. We took a three-week trip to Pennsylvania that summer, where we met members of the Mennonite community and saw their unique society. They loved the Lord and lived a very modest and simple lifestyle. Rachel stayed with a family from the church New Life members attended, or with my mom when our group traveled. One time, my mom bought Rachel a Christmas stocking and enjoyed the week with her newest grandchild while I was on the road.

Although I had lived my whole life in small towns, traveling was enjoyable, and visiting big cities wasn't a culture shock at all. We met a lot of different people and relished the love they showed us. It was a learning experience for me to receive that kind of love and acceptance because I had grown up not believing people or accepting their love. I still had a difficult time trusting other people outside the group I traveled with. But touring with them and meeting wonderful Christians everywhere made me feel that I wasn't alone, and I learned how to receive their love and graciousness. I remember being scared about being around a lot of people I did not know, and having to push myself out of my comfort zone by trusting strangers. But I was young enough to adapt to change.

I realized there was nothing in the old life for me to go back to, but the pull of the group and lifestyle would occasionally whisper in my ear. The street calls out to you, as those who live the life I did like to say, and the lure of addiction and the adrenaline rush of excitement beckoned. But now I knew a different way. The Bible is right when it speaks of sin having pleasure for a season, but there is always a price to pay in the end. In some cases, the end result of sin is physical death.

I had everything to gain at New Life and nothing to lose as I moved from death to new life in Jesus Christ. Looking back now, I can see the girl that left New Life was not the same one who showed up with no hope and no future. Even my family noticed the change. God had a different plan for me than the street did.

Chapter 6

YOUTH WITH
A MISSION

I had only finished the ninth grade when I entered New Life. However, I did eventually get my high school equivalency (GED) about eight months later. I struggled with math and science but enjoyed English and social studies. New Life's Phase I program focused on healing, not acting out, and learning to live a new way. Phase Two helped me build a solid foundation for my life by memorizing scriptures and learning to live by Godly principles. Phase Three taught me how to manage money, prioritize my spending, and the importance of giving to the Lord through tithing. After living at New Life for a little over a year, I graduated from Phase Three of their program, which included working a couple of days a week at a cleaning business that partnered with them.

During Phase Three, I became friends with Deb and Doug Tunney, who had a window cleaning business and had started caring for pregnant girls in Manchester. They worked with some of the New Life girls and had been with a ministry called Youth With A Mission. I was intrigued by the work of the organization and began thinking about joining them.

Youth With A Mission is a global gathering of people from many cultures, age groups, and Christian traditions. They were dedicated to serving Jesus throughout the world. Also known as YWAM (pronounced "WHY-wham"), they are bound by the common purpose of knowing God and making Him known. YWAM is a discipleship and ministry program and seemed to be a good next step for me as I wanted to go into ministry and share the gospel with others in need. Doug and Deb thought it would be a good fit for me—and I agreed.

As one of the first graduates of New Life's 18-month program, it was now time to take my "next step." It included saving the money needed to get more training and further my education. With all that I had learned and the changes God had made in me, I knew I could live my life dependent on Jesus and not on drugs or alcohol. A few weeks before graduating from New Life, I began preparing a transition plan, which I was required to present to George, Grace, and the board.

I was nervous about them accepting my idea to go to YWAM. As I expected, George and Grace weren't so sure about my decision. Their hesitancy had mostly to do with me having Rachel and having to juggle raising her with going to school. They wanted me to give back a year at New Life as a staff member after graduating, but I felt like it was not the best environment for Rachel and that I needed a change. They eventually agreed to accept my decision.

Graduation from New Life was low key with no formal ceremony, just a cake and a handful of people. My mom and stepfather, Steve, attended as another girl and I graduated. George and Grace were still hopeful that I would return to New Life as a staff member. Their hope was that I would serve for one year after completing the five-to-six-month YWAM Discipleship Training School (DTS).

So, upon graduation from New Life, I went to YWAM to further my training. It was scary to take this next step, and I left New Life with mixed emotions. I was anxious to leave and excited about going to YWAM in nearby Concord, New Hampshire. Still, it was lonely being out on my own. I needed help with the money required to attend YWAM, so my sister helped raise my financial support, even giving me her rent money to help me take this next step.

Completing DTS would give me more skills to share the Gospel and teach me to be more disciplined in my prayer life. Plus, I wanted to hone my skills in sharing what God had done for me. The DTS course was a full-time commitment consisting of lectures and outreach. During the first phase, students learned more about God and His Word not only in lectures but also from community living and practical training. The outreach phase focused on applying what you learned in the classroom through an intense, cross-cultural experience.

Living in a dorm at YWAM did help in the transition process, and daily life wasn't much different there than at New Life. I did have more freedom and greater choices in whether or not to participate in activities. One time, I chose to skip class, stay in my room, and eat breakfast. A staff member came and called me out for skipping class. It made me realize I still had a lot to learn about making good choices!

I was the only single mom at YWAM, but there were other people there who had kids, as well as families and couples of all ages. At first, I was uneasy having men around, but I learned how to be friends with them. I loved the new environment, being around different groups, and learning new skills. People were kind to me, and everyone helped take care of Rachel. It was easy to have conversations with the other students, and I felt like I belonged to this unique "family within a family."

In addition to studying evangelism, our team learned to dance and used that artistic outlet to break down language barriers and communicate the gospel. Because I love to dance, I really enjoyed developing this skill and utilizing it to share God's Good News. After dancing, we would go out into the crowds in places we traveled, such as Boston, Philadelphia, and New Jersey. I loved traveling to new places and wanted to tell everyone I met what Jesus had done for me. It was a thrill leading people to Christ, and the training I had received at New Life and YWAM put me at ease in sharing my story and the gospel message.

Like many works of faith, YWAM began with a vision. In June of 1956, Loren Cunningham, a 20-year-old student from the United States, spent part of his summer break in Nassau, the Bahamas, touring with a singing group. Three years earlier, he had participated in an outreach to Mexico as a teen and preached the gospel in broken Spanish. He and his team were amazed that God could use them to reach another culture and win people for Jesus. The seeds for the YWAM ministry were planted that day. Today, YWAM continues its work of preparing and sending people out into the world's mission fields, sharing the love of Jesus Christ, primarily through prayer and evangelism.

Although YWAM's training was focused on sending graduates into the mission field, they didn't pressure me to go in that direction. They encouraged me to go back to New Life, where they felt that my gifts could be best utilized. I resisted that counsel because I was unsure what my role would be upon returning. I just felt like it wasn't right for me at that time, even though it had been just what I needed when I entered their program. Strangely, I also felt that if I returned to New Life at the age of 21, I would die an unmarried old maid and be there for the rest of my life!

Now that Rachel was two, I also didn't feel New Life would be a suitable environment for her either, and I didn't want to raise her there. I now realize how ridiculous that thinking was because it would have been a totally safe environment for her. I felt in limbo and was somewhat discouraged because everyone who graduated YWAM with me had a mission, but I felt like I didn't. YWAM offered a school of evangelism after the DTS training, but it cost about $2,000, and I didn't have the money to attend. YWAM didn't ask me to put together a transition plan because everyone who graduated from DTS either went on to the evangelism training or out into the mission field. Neither one was an option for me.

One of the skills I learned at YWAM was how to share my testimony publicly, when we visited jails, spoke at youth prisons, and chatted with the inmates. It was scary, but the fear was not from the environment but from having to talk in front of people and share my story. People came to Christ as a result, and that made it easier the next time. I didn't know then that this training would prepare me for other opportunities down the road.

Looking back now, I probably should have gone back to New Life. Instead, I bounced around a bit before returning home to live with my mom. I got a job at a factory making stuffed animals and tried to get my own apartment. However, I made too much money to qualify for low-income housing. Both my mom and I agreed that moving back with her was just temporary and that I needed to go out on my own.

Afraid that I would return to making bad choices and go down the wrong path again, the New Life staff wasn't happy with my decision to return home. They were right to be concerned because the safety canopies I enjoyed at both New Life and YWAM were gone once I was on my own. The New Life program had an 80 percent success rate with graduates, but they were always aware of the 20 percent that failed. Those who failed usually ended up dead or back in jail. But after going through New Life and YWAM's training programs, I was confident I could succeed because I did not want to go back to the old life. I longed to share the gospel with others and felt I now had the tools to succeed and get back on track if and when I made mistakes. I also had the phone numbers of people I could call for help and no longer felt alone in my journey.

I had initially given up all my freedom when I entered New Life. Slowly I got that freedom back, and now had to make all my own decisions. The New Life staff would check in with me occasionally, and I also utilized a self-check-in with them. After I left YWAM, I kind of lost track of the people there as many of my fellow students went off to the mission field. Little did I know a different "mission field" awaited me just around the corner.

Even though I had the "head knowledge" about the dangers of such a relationship, it was hard to apply. That was something I never thought I'd struggle with. So, Bill and I decided to get married because things had progressed physically, and I was three months pregnant. Bill also loved Rachel and appreciated how I mothered her. He saw something different there because he didn't see that kind of relationship elsewhere. Bill was 18, I was 22, and although we never really formally dated, we got married within a year after meeting. Even though Bill was only 18, he was older than his years street-wise but had a lot to learn about responsibility. Like me, Bill was a survivor.

Without my mom's blessing, Bill and I were married in April 1987 by a Justice of the Peace in nearby Keene, at a funeral home of all places. We didn't realize it was a funeral home at the time. It was just the address for the Justice of the Peace when we looked him up. He married us in the chapel, but my mom refused to come because she thought I was making a mistake by not dumping Bill.

We didn't have any formal witnesses, just the two of us, an attendant, and the justice of the peace. Although I would have liked to have had my mom there, we didn't care that no one from either of our families attended. My mom felt us getting married was wrong, but I think we were using each other to survive, because of our similar backgrounds. We both needed each other, and I guess I felt that it was just the next logical step for us. We didn't belong anywhere, but we belonged together. In Bill, I saw someone that I had a lot in common with. He was looking for a relationship and a family because his life at home was rough.

At first, I think my family was praying I would back out of the relationship with Bill, but they softened to him. They didn't like the fact that Bill wasn't living as a Christian, but within hours of us getting married, they began changing their perception of him.

My sisters decorated our car with wedding bells, and we went to his dad's and then off to a hotel for our short honeymoon. Because neither of us had our own place, after the honeymoon, Bill's mom let us stay with her in a mobile home and eventually gifted it to us. We had to thoroughly clean and fix it up. The floors had to be replaced and she had animals, so it needed to be remodeled and cleaned. Bill's mom moved into an apartment with her other son and his girlfriend when we took possession of the trailer.

About a year after we were married, Bill came to Christ in a pretty dramatic change. Our pastor came by every week and won my husband over to Christ by serving and loving us and doing practical things like installing a sink and helping Bill work on the trailer. Bill began reading his Bible, dumped his beer down the drain, and started going to church. He began taking the leadership role in our home and helping out at church. Bill needed a lot of spiritual guidance, and the love and selfless giving the pastor had shown him won him over.

Bill had come from a Missionary Alliance Church background due to the influence of a family that used to take him to church. He had accepted Christ as a child at a Billy Graham crusade, but didn't follow through on his decision. It was similar to what I had gone through. But his recommitment was genuine and helped knit us more closely together as a couple. It wasn't easy, and we struggled as many young couples do, but God was with us as we began our married life.

As Bill continued growing in his faith, he began to more fully understand why my relationship with Jesus was more important to me than my relationship with him. He was learning to pray and put his faith into practice. He read Rachel a Bible story every night and learned a lot about Jesus and the Bible from those children's stories. Bill wanted to tell people about Christ. As a result, a lot of his friends drifted away. He continued struggling to find work but eventually landed a job at a sawmill. My old Chevy Citation had died, and we didn't replace it, so Bill had to get rides to work since we didn't have transportation. He was just 19, a new believer, and zealous for his faith. As a result, he took a lot of heat at work for witnessing to co-workers and bringing his Bible to the job.

My family was excited when our son, Matthew, was born in October 1987. It was a much different reaction from my family than I got over Rachel's birth. For me, his birth was awesome and very different. In addition to the excitement, we had a baby shower and received a lot of gifts. The delivery was much easier for me than when Rachel was born, and I was also more emotionally stable than before. Of course, I had Bill praying with me and supporting me emotionally, too.

I was in the hospital about two days after Matthew was born and then went home. Initially, we planned to name our new son Peter James, but at the last minute, Bill looked at me and I looked at him. I said, "What do you think about Matthew Allen?" We both instantly loved the name, and he became Matthew Allen. My family celebrated with us, and Rachel, who was five at the time, loved her baby brother. Bill was terrific, helping out by cleaning the house and doing other things as I recovered from giving birth. We tried to keep Rachel's routines the same, keeping such traditions as reading to her at night.

Having a newborn in the house wasn't a problem for me. I was the youngest in my family and had spent a lot of time around my sisters' kids. Of course, Bill was happy to have a son to carry on the family name. Because we had a newborn, I stayed home raising both Matthew and Rachel. Without my income, we had trouble making ends meet. Life was so busy, and I would babysit other people's kids to make a little extra money.

Sometimes when there wasn't enough work at the sawmill they would shut down for a few days, further cutting our income. It was a hard life; work was sparse, and we lived frugally in the trailer. We had no cable television, ate a lot of macaroni and cheese, and did odd jobs to bring in more income. All during that time, we continued to tithe, trusting God to provide all our needs. We ate supper at the table together as a family and enjoyed the routine that I had learned at New Life and YWAM. We were living one day at a time by God's grace.

Bill wasn't used to having such a stable routine, so that was an adjustment for him. He did not know how to respond to it but enjoyed being married. Because he had grown up in a volatile environment, my husband also had trust issues, as I had when I first went to New Life. Bill loved having and being part of a family, especially around the holidays, and learned that he could trust me. I had a harder time adjusting to married life. I felt trapped, and that I had betrayed the Lord by what I now saw as marrying someone outside of my faith. I was constantly second-guessing my decision to marry and beating myself up, wondering how God could bless my disobedience. I felt trapped like I had chains binding me because I thought God would never allow me to be in ministry again and that I had settled for less than His best.

For a time, the guilt was overwhelming and blocked out the fact that God could still use me. I wasn't feeling blessed and now see that my focus was on myself and not on God. Mostly, I fought these internal battles through prayer and by being plugged into a church community. Every time the doors were open, we were there. A couple of years later, when we started doing ministry together, the guilt lifted. I sensed that God could indeed use me again. I really appreciated that Bill wanted to serve the Lord and that we could do so together.

Chapter 8

TOUGH TIMES

About a year after starting at the sawmill, Bill lost his job and was without steady work for a couple of years. Because the economy was so bad in our area, he worked odd jobs, sometimes at the Quaker Oats plant in Vermont, which he got through a temp agency. Bill was miserable at times, as men often are when they don't feel they are providing for their families. It was tough for us financially, but I was used to living without much. I turned to prayer for God's provision, cleaned houses, babysat, and did other odd jobs to bring in more money. That two-year period, which felt like four, was rough, and we were forced to move into another low-income apartment. We called it eking out a living. It was miserable, I was depressed a lot, but we made it work. God was faithful, sometimes providing in the strangest ways!

We helped manage the apartments where we lived and did some of the needed maintenance and painting. One day, the owners decided to replace all the toilets in the complex and throw the old ones out. But instead of doing so, they gave us the nearly-new 27 commodes they were replacing. I got an idea as I was praying for the money we needed to buy groceries.

"Bill," I told my husband, "these toilets are in perfect condition. Just collect them and put them in our yard!"

The look he gave me said it all. "Are you out of your mind?" Reluctantly, he did it.

"Phyllis, we have toilets all over our yard," he said one day in exasperation. "I don't know what I'm gonna do with all these toilets if I can't get rid of them!"

Bill then called a friend and began asking around. "Does anyone need a toilet?"

His thinking was that we would sell them piecemeal. As I was praying, one of Bill's friends called him back, saying he knew someone at a camp that needed them.

"We want to buy all the toilets," the person from The Takodah YMCA camp said. He told Bill they had to have water-saving toilets, and the ones we had were exactly what they needed. Bill was stunned and negotiated a deal with them to take all 27 for $300, which was a lot of money at the time. The income was enough to buy groceries and bridge the gap between jobs. It was a humorous lesson for us about God's provision, and a reminder that He always provides for his children and those in ministry.

The kids were continuing to grow, Rachel was especially thrilled to have a dad, and they became really close. Settling down was good for her, and she loved the security of living in a family. She really took to Bill and only got scared when we argued in front of her. Sadly, we argued frequently, mostly about money and time. Bill was gone a lot, sometimes working 16-hour days, and I would be left with the kids. I felt that he didn't understand the team concept of marriage, and I wondered why he couldn't help me more when he wasn't working. Back then, he thought it was a woman's job to take care of the house and kids and have dinner on the table. However, Bill later came to understand my need for him to help out around the house and carry some of the load.

One day out of the blue, Rachel's birth father decided he wanted to be a part of her life again. I never learned why, but later discovered that my mom had been keeping him in the loop about us. When he found out we were nearby, he said he wanted to see his daughter. I was nervous about that because he had never understood how to be her dad. But he said he wanted to be a part of her life, got a lawyer, and proceeded to take legal action. Adding to that stress was the fact that we had to get a pro-bono lawyer because we couldn't afford an attorney to help us navigate through the legal maze. Bill got upset that I didn't insist on child support, but I didn't want to accept the help from Rachel's dad, who had never been there for her. I thought that taking his money would give him more leverage over us. However, I did agree to accept some child support from him after the attorneys got involved. The lawyers hammered out an agreement, and we simply had to present it to the judge and say we approved.

Rachel's dad won visitation rights to see his five-year-old daughter when we settled out of court. It was tough on her. The reemergence of her dad into our lives also caused some conflict between me and Bill. Part of that tension was over the fact that Bill had wanted to adopt Rachel but couldn't because her biological father didn't want to let her go.

The lawyer representing Rachel's dad wouldn't listen to our plea to start the visitation process slowly so Rachel could adjust to it. Instead, she had to visit for two weeks the first time, and she cried and would not sleep for most of her visit. I did not do a very good job explaining the situation to her, and years later, she told me she thought she would have to live with her dad permanently. After that incident, he never took her for that long again, and the visitations began petering out. Eventually, those visitations evolved into two weeks a year and every other Christmas.

Bill initially thought Rachel was betraying me by visiting her dad. But she really had no say in the matter because it was court ordered. Bill realized that Rachel's dad would use her to get to me, and he was good about protecting me from that. The visits pretty much continued until Rachel was 16 and decided she didn't want to go anymore.

The episode with Rachel's dad caught us off guard because I'd had no contact with him. I was also angry and hurt that my mom had been talking to him behind my back. Frankly, I wished the whole thing would just go away, but it was a learning opportunity for me as I prayed and asked God, "Why is this happening? Why now?" The Lord said to me, "She's mine. You have to trust Me. You can't trust in people, but you have to trust in Me." I also learned to have compassion for absentee fathers and understand what they go through. However, that lesson was slow to come.

Every time I had to let Rachel visit her dad, I remembered how he had treated me. I had to learn to trust God to take care of my daughter all over again. At the same time, I also realized that people change and maybe her dad finally understood what a gift he had in his daughter. To his credit, Bill handled all the visitation negotiations so I did not have to deal with it. For the most part, the visits were okay, but Rachel was confused by shuttling back and forth. She was too young to understand going from a Christian to a non-Christian home and the contrast between the two lifestyles.

While all of this was happening, Bill and I had been debating about whether to have another child, and I finally told him, "I'm ready." What I meant was that I was emotionally ready. However, we were not prepared money-wise and never even discussed the financial ramifications of having another child. Nevertheless, we proceeded, and the birth process was much easier this time around. I was comfortable and settled and it was less stressful for me emotionally. I could really enjoy this pregnancy and was excited about having another child. In addition, I wasn't as sick as I had been with the previous pregnancies.

I remember the day in 1990 when Vanessa was born. Bill and I dropped Rachel off at school, went to the hospital, and I had the baby while she was at school. Bill stayed with me much of the time, and I went home the next day. While I was gone, Bill had cleaned the house and bought groceries and a plant for me. With Vanessa, three-year-old Matthew, and seven-year-old Rachel, our family was now complete.

While we were thrilled to welcome Vanessa into our family, having three kids with no full-time income was emotionally stressful for us. We got emergency food stamps but didn't get any other government assistance, not even unemployment. I don't remember why, but it may have been that Bill hadn't worked enough within the system to qualify for benefits. We struggled over the decision of even getting food stamps, wondering if it reflected a lack of faith in God's provision. A lot of people we knew thought it was a "sin" to ask for government assistance because the ethic was "if you don't work, you don't eat." That mindset definitely influenced us, but we eventually realized we had to provide for our children, no matter what anyone said.

When Vanessa was about 10 months old, Bill landed a job as a janitor and handyman at C&S Wholesale Grocers in nearby Brattleboro, Vermont. It was a great job and boosted Bill's confidence because he was now able to provide for his family. Even though it was an excellent opportunity, Bill was upset at first because it was a second shift job. He didn't like leaving me home alone without a car. Bill would leave at 3:30 in the afternoon and sometimes work until noon the next day. We rarely saw each other and it was physically taxing on both of us.

In addition, Vanessa had pneumonia three times during her first year of life, adding to his concerns. When that happened, I often had to wait for him to get home from work and then take her to the doctor. They eventually discovered that she had asthma, which was causing pneumonia. While he struggled at first with the new schedule, Bill obeyed God. As a result, he matured a lot as a man and father. I loved having him on second shift because I got to spend a lot of time with the kids and nurture our family. We adjusted our schedules and had our big meal together as a family in the afternoon before Bill left for work.

Bill gradually moved up at C&S to become part of the first landscaping and snow removal crew there. He loved being outside and doing that kind of work. Little did we know that eventually he would leverage that experience into starting our own landscaping business. We also moved out of our low-income housing and rented a house in Keene, about 20 miles from Bill's job. In another of God's provision miracles, 32 people applied for the house, but we apparently stood out to the owners who approved us. It was definitely a step up, with better schools and a nicer community, as well as being closer to Bill's job. The job also allowed us to buy a car to ease the burden of getting around. Bill took the car to work because my sister-in-law lived nearby and would take me anywhere if an emergency arose or the kids needed something.

We had looked everywhere for a car but had very little money and no credit. A friend from church named Ed called us up one day and asked, "Are you looking for a car?" He had apparently heard about our need at church or from my mom. He picked us up and took us to see the car. As we talked, he asked Bill if he ever considered mowing lawns on the side. "I think that would be good for you," Ed told him, almost seeming to prophesize about our future. "Are you kidding me?" Bill responded. "A teenager does that!"

Even though we brushed it off at the time, Bill and I never forgot that conversation. Ed seemed to sense that landscaping was to be a part of God's plan for us. We decided to buy the car Ed showed us, and after making a couple of small payments, he ended up giving it to us. "I feel that the Lord is telling me to give you the car," he said. It marked the first time someone had really given something to us and served as another great reminder of God's provision.

Chapter 9

PHELPS LANDSCAPE

After working at C&S for a year, Bill moved to first shift as part of the maintenance and landscaping team and got a significant pay raise to boot. He liked being outdoors and was in the right place at the right time as C&S expanded their landscaping work. His new hours were 4:30 a.m. to 2:00 p.m. However, he worked a lot of overtime, which was somewhat expected if you wanted to advance in the company.

As part of the first landscaping crew at C&S, he learned all the manual labor phases of the business, including everything from sharpening lawn mower blades to properly mowing a field. He also learned about snow removal. In New Hampshire, landscaping stops in the winter, so snow removal was essential in keeping money coming in during the off-season.

Bill fit in well with the maintenance team. He enjoyed the landscaping work, which set the stage for our future. When he wasn't working overtime or on side jobs, he liked being home in the afternoon and it was a pleasant change for me having Bill around during the day.

With his new hours and added responsibilities, the biggest change in our lives was two-fold: The number of hours Bill was working and the boost in his confidence. The winter snowplowing often meant he was gone a lot, working well over 40 hours a week. Because some roads, like Chesterfield Hill, were treacherous during the winter, the snow removal crews stayed in one location for days at a time. The company would put them up at an area motel until the storm blew through and they finished clearing the snow. While it was hard for me to have him gone for extended periods, Bill was paid for the entire time he was gone, even while sleeping.

Bill's confidence was boosted by the fact that he was able to provide for our family and acquired a good work ethic, something he didn't learn growing up. He was able to help discipline the kids when they complained about their homework and was free to attend their sporting events. I don't know how he found time, but he also coached Matthew's hockey and Vanessa's softball teams. There were times he would literally come home from days on the road and go right to a hockey game. I knew he was exhausted, but I helped out as much as possible by paying the bills and keeping the house so he had time to spend with the kids. We were also connecting with others in both the community and schools. It was a quiet time in our lives, a time of learning and settling into a comfortable routine.

Despite the long hours, I made the best of every work shift Bill had at C&S, sometimes helping out as well. They would hire me to fill in on the phones or assist with billing or auditing on a per-diem basis when someone was sick or on maternity leave.

Getting into the landscaping business was a tremendous learning experience and led to another milestone in our lives. One day Bill came to me and said, "I'm really thinking about starting my own business, but I'm afraid." That fear came from the security we had working for a large company with its insurance and 401(k) benefits. But we began putting out proposals to test the waters and see if we could land some side business.

There were a lot of reasons Bill wanted to strike out on his own. People in our part of the country aren't churchgoers, and he was getting worn down from the negativity as he shared his faith at work. Many people look down their noses at "church people." It was getting more and more challenging to maintain his testimony among workers who wanted to go drinking or visit strip clubs after work or during lunch.

Bill had been doing landscaping jobs on the side while working full-time at C&S, and we had some extra income from my fill-in jobs. Among our side job clients was the vice president of C&S. He had asked Bill to landscape his property even though C&S had their own landscaping division.

"Let's put aside this extra income for a year and consider if we can do this," I said to him, and that's what we did. We socked away the extra money for about a year, continuing to pray about whether this was the direction God was leading. Word got around, we landed additional clients, and people were coming to Bill and asking him to do landscaping for them.

Working for the vice president of C&S was huge and a good source of referrals for us. A lot of the other company VPs saw the job Bill did and wanted him to work on their landscaping. After submitting a bid for their five complexes, we also landed a mowing contract from a low-income housing facility. This was huge and seemed to be a good sign as the doors continued opening for us to go out on our own.

We officially launched Phelps Landscape in 2000. Giving up a regular paycheck and the security it provided was difficult.

Even though we had set aside "seed money" to launch our business, we tapped into our 401(k) to buy equipment, a decision we later regretted. Money was tight, and we had to cut back on some things, but it was not a huge change for us or our lifestyle. I admit I was terrified at the beginning, hoping that this was the way God was moving us in starting our own business. Even though I trusted God, it was difficult giving up our insurance and benefits, especially while raising a family. But we firmly believed God was leading, so we moved forward. It was also an adjustment working for Bill because the job could be very demanding.

With Bill in the field, we didn't see each other much, and I would often go in at night to do my work because it was much quieter. The first year was rough as the snow plowing part of our business was down. It is a very competitive arena, and if you aren't already established, it's tough to break into the market. We had trouble landing contracts for that type of work until we had made a name for ourselves. Only the money we made from fall cleanups helped get us through the winter. I did my best to support Bill, giving him the encouragement he needed and helping out where I could.

We had been in business a little over a year when the world stopped turning on September 11, 2001. Like everyone else in America, we watched the events of the day unfold on television. Living only about 200 miles from New York City, we knew people who had friends working in the Twin Towers. It was a surreal day for us. Many people, especially college students, showed up at our house, packing my living room to follow the day's events. They were scared and wanted to be with friends and loved ones. Our house became a magnet and made them feel safe.

It was eerie for us, too, because we knew The Brooklyn Tabernacle's pastor, Jim Cymbala. The renowned church is only five

miles from Ground Zero across the East River via the Brooklyn Bridge. Pastor Cymbala later told us that people flooded his
church, and others, after 9/11, looking for comfort and reas-
surance after the day's horrifying events. Although we didn't
personally know anyone who died that terrible day, many people
in our area did.

Apart from 9/11, we continued building our business, raising our family, and enjoying life. Matthew lost interest in school,
struggling with low grades during his senior year, and wound up
attending night school.

Rachel started college in 2001 at the age of 18. I remember
her telling me at the beginning, "Mom, we just don't have the
money for college. We can't do this." I told her to go until we ran
out of money, but we never did. God provided each step of the
way through loans and scholarships.

In the first couple of years, Phelps Landscape had two part-
time workers and me. We hired family members and college
students, and I raked leaves by myself, vowing afterward to never
do that again! It was back-breaking work, and I was left alone in a
field with leaves up to my knees. It just wasn't for me! I needed to
be in the office. We did a lot of advertising in the local newspaper
and on the radio and would scour the paper looking for jobs to
bid on. We stayed up late, putting together and submitting bids,
and business increased in 2003, our third year as a company.
Even C&S gave some of their landscape and snow removal work
to our company when they had more than they could handle.

With our success, we were able to give back to the community. We donated to the local Christian school and sponsored
area sports teams. As our name got out there, Phelps Landscape
continued growing. In 2005, we were able to buy our house. That
was an amazing blessing, given our backgrounds and how we

had been raised. But people didn't remember where we had come from. They focused on the "wow" of our lives and how God had changed us. Local churches were very supportive and helped us as we built bridges to others in the faith community. "Good for you guys," people would say as they recognized me in the grocery store every week.

Bill went back and got his GED in 2006, partially to set an example for our son, Matthew, and demonstrate to him the importance of getting a good education. Matthew also struggled with depression, and I prayed a lot for him to work through it and the anger that seemed to have a grip on him. Matthew was a tremendous help to the landscaping business, even though it could get frustrating for him.

Rachel graduated Cum Laude that same year, becoming the first of my mom's 19 grandchildren to graduate from college. She majored in business management, taking an extra year to finish because she had gotten married in 2005.

My daughter Vanessa attended college for one year and discovered it just wasn't for her. She got a job working with her sister at an insurance company and began dating the pastor's son. Ben had graduated from the Teen Challenge program. After a four-year courtship, they married several years later, and he owns a successful bike shop in our community.

In 2006, we began working in a marriage ministry in our church. We were blessed to be able to attend training in Hawaii! The ministry work itself took place in home small groups and Bible studies, which we not only led but helped facilitate. We utilized materials from *The Love Dare* book, which was popularized in the movie "Fireproof." In the film, a couple seeks to rescue their marriage from the brink of divorce and temptation using *The Love Dare* as their guide. The daily devotionals steer couples through the challenges of developing a healthy, committed marriage in a world that doesn't value spiritual and Christian principles.

We also led couples on a Weekend to Remember retreat, an outreach of Family Life Ministries. These romantic weekends helped couples invest in and strengthen their marriages, no matter what state their relationship was in. It offered a chance to get away and return to what matters most. What Bill and I liked about the retreats was it gave couples practical tools to resolve conflict in healthy and productive ways and learn how to forgive. But the getaways weren't counseling sessions or group discussions, so attendees didn't have to worry about sharing intimate details about their marriage with total strangers. We were awed by how God touched and healed marriages through these ministry programs.

At our peak in 2008 and 2009, Phelps Landscape was grossing about $400,000 a year and had between eight and 10 workers. Never forgetting where we had come from, we often hired people that had a tough time making it. If someone didn't have a way to work, we'd let them use one of our trucks. Bill also provided all of our workers with cellphones. We helped them with groceries if they had a need and adjusted our summer hours to avoid working in the heat of the day. We created a family atmosphere at work and threw a big Christmas party every year. People work better if you treat them with respect, and as a result, our workers were extremely loyal to both our company and to us. People trusted us, and God was growing our business!

"Mom, we are so blessed," Rachel told me one day, humbled by the way God was working in our family. We were able to take our kids on vacation and enjoy the fruits of our success. Bill and I took cruises to Mexico, the Bahamas, Jamaica, and the

Caribbean, plus side trips to Hampton Beach and Maine.

During this time in our lives, we were in the process of switching churches for a variety of reasons. However, we ended up returning to our original church after Bill's accident. Life was normal and busy. We had family members over for a swimming party on Sunday just before heading out on vacation. Little did we know that our lives would radically change the next day.

Chapter 10

LIFE IS GOOD

Bill's accident in 2009 led us into a place where we didn't know God existed. Pastor Cymbala often talks about the shadow of death. I had been there before in my previous life but didn't realize until then how one split second can shatter your life. I didn't understand God's timing regarding the accident because we were serving the Lord in ministry. It prompted me to ask God, "What's going on?"

I never questioned the "why" of the accident, but was asking God what was next for us and where He was leading. Nonetheless, Bill and I both went through a time of anger. His is ongoing, while mine lasted about a year. Our lives were shattered in a moment. Everything familiar and comfortable was taken away in the blink of an eye. I was angry and mourned over not being able to say goodbye to the man I loved and had married. Bill, the man I had been with for so long, was now totally different.

In the days after the wreck, I would wake up thinking it was all a nightmare. I remember taking a shower and not being able to feel either the hot or cold water, even when it was on full blast. I was emotionally and mentally numb much of the time, in shock and tuning out. People would talk to me and I wouldn't hear them. What I heard sounded like the "wah, wah, wah" of adults talking in the Charlie Brown cartoons.

During the time after Bill's wreck, some people thought (and said) that God allowed the accident to deal with our pride over what we had accomplished, the material things we enjoyed, and that our children were doing so well. Some of their hostility was motivated by jealousy, and sadly, some came from church people. Other caustic remarks came from people Bill had worked with or from clients. Comments like, "Well, he won't do that again," referring to Bill riding his motorcycle without a helmet, were especially hurtful. I got some hateful emails from some people I thought were friends. Those were especially hard.

Spiritually, the Lord had to step in and minister to me emotionally. Other people often didn't know what to say but they were there for us in practical ways, such as providing meals or just sitting with me at the hospital. There were always people I could ask to help, but they often showed up without me even asking. God sent His angels to us through His people on more than one occasion.

In addition, there were a lot of people in the church encouraging and praying for us. I leaned on the Lord, my pastor, and even my doctor for strength. I can recall what they said, where I was, and what I experienced.

Despite the encouragement, all I could do through my tears and prayers was sing. "Bless the Lord, oh my soul, and all that is within me, bless His Holy Name," was all I could say. I knew I needed to have God walk me through this, which He did. God heals the brokenness and splices the pieces of our lives back together. As my granddaughter reminded me one day while riding in the car, "Jesus fixes broken hearts." Gradually, He did rebuild all the broken places in our lives.

Prayer has always been at the center of our lives and the ministries we've been in. It was prayer that brought us through the accident. We didn't stop serving God despite the new obstacles and challenges He allowed into our lives. Thankfully, our marriage was strong enough to endure this challenge. I've often thought that had Bill's motorcycle wreck happened in the early years of our marriage, we probably wouldn't have stayed together. I think that is because we didn't have a solid Christian foundation, and my walk in the Lord was not as strong then. I would have had to give a lot of attention to the kids who would have been much younger. I don't believe I could have handled it all.

But God knew, and such is His timing and grace. As all that pain ended, life began settling down again. I realized that we wouldn't be involved in our current ministry and seeing lives changed without Bill's accident. Through it all, I felt God was there for us. I think He was much like the fourth man in the fire in the story of Shadrach, Meshach, and Abednego from the book of Daniel.

"You have a good name," I remember our pastor telling us after the accident. He reminded me that our house was built on the Lord, and we would survive Bill's motorcycle wreck. "Your name is hidden with Jesus," he told us. After the accident, that was all that was left.

Chapter 11

PICKING UP
THE PIECES

We were active in our church's marriage ministry and enjoyed sharing biblically-based tools to strengthen relationships. Part of our excitement was teaching couples what the Bible says about the different roles men and women have in leadership. It was such a joy helping each member discover their place in the body of Christ. We were working our way through Pastor Cymbala's video and book series, "When God's People Pray" when Bill's accident ended our involvement. A separate Bible study home group also eventually fell apart as we weren't able to continue attending during Bill's recovery.

In addition to the marriage ministry, Bill and I also worked with troubled young people from a nearby youth detention center. I had gotten to know some of their parents from our local sports teams or our business. We had hosted several of these young people in our home before the accident, offering them spiritual guidance and mentoring. We continued doing so during the months of Bill's hospital stays and rehab. Looking back, it seems like we always had someone who needed help staying in our home. After the accident, just our son, Matthew, and two Christian young men from the church stayed with us. They helped with some household projects such as painting, mowing the lawn, running errands, and working in our business.

In August 2009, just two days after Bill left rehab, my two-year-old granddaughter slipped into diabetic shock. Technically known as severe hypoglycemia or low blood sugar, it was so bad the doctors couldn't even get a needle into her collapsing veins. So, at 11:00 at night, I was heading back to Dartmouth in what seemed like a bad dream. I felt like Job, overwhelmed with everything happening at once. *I feel so defeated, having to go back to the hospital,* I thought. "Mom, I'm not even over dad's accident yet," Rachel said. The doctors were able to stabilize my granddaughter, and she was diagnosed with Juvenile Diabetes.

Part of feeling overwhelmed when my granddaughter was rushed to Dartmouth was trying to run Phelps Landscape on my own after Bill's accident. I tried fulfilling current contracts, doing some of the work myself, and even enlisted my brother and a friend to work for us. My son couldn't see continuing the business without his dad, and he didn't want the burden of running it himself. Without Bill's day-to-day, hands-on guidance, some of our workers would claim to begin a job when that wasn't true, or they wouldn't finish it if they had started it. The quality of the work suffered, as did our business reputation. But Bill's recovery was more important to me than the business, and I handled things robotically as they came up. I found that I had to bury my emotions and deal with each day's events as they occurred. While the doctors had been clear that Bill would never fully recover from his accident, I was always hoping and praying for a miracle. I longed for life to return to the way it was before his motorcycle wreck.

We didn't know anyone capable or interested in taking over Phelps Landscape. None of our competitors offered to buy us out either, perhaps because our reputation had suffered and the business was quickly falling apart. My son-in-law was one candidate to run our business, but that would have meant him giving up a good job as a buyer at C&S, and that just wasn't feasible.

After struggling for about a year, some customers started pulling out of contracts with us because we failed to fulfill our obligations. Other clients did not renew when their agreements expired, and some clients were waiting to see if Bill would return. We stopped pursuing new contracts because I did not have the time. Eventually, we had to sell equipment to pay the bills, and some of our trucks and other assets were repossessed. Many members of our crew left for better jobs because they saw the writing on the wall. Phelps Landscape officially folded in 2011. It took me about three years to get over the pain of losing the business and realizing I had to get a job to provide income for our family.

Losing our business was just one factor that made 2011 especially rough for us. We also lost our home after the business income dried up. We filed a lawsuit that year against the company that employed the driver involved in Bill's accident. We weren't out to get rich, only to recoup the cost of paying the hospital bills while providing for Bill's aftercare, including his at-home and subsequent outpatient physical therapy.

The legal process began when my brother-in-law and the detective working the accident case met me at the hospital shortly after the accident. The detective gave me a copy of the police report. My brother-in-law advised us to get a lawyer and sue for damages as well as medical care expenses. Although he couldn't give us any legal advice, the case detective seemed to agree that we had a good claim against the driver. The police report confirmed that the driver was totally at fault for the accident. Still, the company that employed him fought the lawsuit for about 18 months. They came after us personally, even attacking our marriage based on the fact that we had gotten some counseling from our pastor. They also tried to say they weren't liable because Bill wasn't wearing a helmet, even though New Hampshire does not have a mandatory helmet law. One potential juror, who was a policeman, walked out during jury selection, saying he couldn't be impartial because Bill wasn't wearing a helmet. The lawyers for the company interviewed our doctor. He admitted that Bill had been on pain medications before the accident due to a previous back injury.

In my view, they made the trial more about us and less about the driver who caused the accident. He was on his cellphone at the time and failed to stop at a red light before turning right. However, those facts were never introduced into the trial, so the jury didn't get that information. To this day, I don't know why our attorneys didn't insist those details be introduced as evidence. The driver was also scheduled to testify, but we never got that far. Our lawyers also allowed the opposing attorneys to make Bill not wearing a helmet the focal point of the trial instead of focusing on the van driver's actions.

The jury trial lasted only three days, but they were grueling morning to evening sessions. Our lawyers told us that the panel was split and that we should settle. The jury awarded us $900,000 and I was shocked when our lawyers advised us to take it. I still feel our attorneys did not do a good job representing us and talked us into an early settlement. Despite the $900,000 award, we only received $250,000 while still facing $600,000 in medical bills. The attorneys got one-third of the judgment, and we settled with the hospital for the remaining $300,000. I was so overwhelmed emotionally. I just wanted the trial to end. "God, just get me through the day," was my daily cry to Him.

There was a bizarre twist in the case. The lawyer we initially hired contracted an intestinal disease and died from brain cancer. He literally called me from his death bed, saying, "I'm going to get you the help you deserve, but please take care of my wife." The insurance company and a new team of attorneys wound up giving a portion of our settlement to his widow. That was not something I remember agreeing to, but it may have been stipulated in one of the countless papers I signed. Either way, I felt we got the short end of the deal. What made it even more difficult was the emotional turmoil of sitting through the trial after everything else we had gone through. Looking back on the entire ordeal, I realized that, metaphorically, not only was Bill on that motorcycle, but so was our entire family, business, and livelihood.

Despite the hospital bills, the less-than-expected settlement, and losing our home and business, we were glad to see the trial end. Looking back now, I often wonder if a larger monetary award might have ruined us. It may have led us away from the Lord or the ministry we are involved in today. While God provided for us financially every step of the way, it was hard to understand why events unfolded the way they did. I'm convinced that someday the Lord will show us the reason.

In addition to the trial, in 2011, my dad died from stomach cancer. We had been in touch through the years, but I had only seen him about five times. He had called me to tell me how sorry he was to hear about Bill's accident, and I had made plans to visit him. He died just one week before my scheduled trip. During the last time I spoke with him, less than a week before he died, he asked for my forgiveness, which I gave him, and I begged him to make his peace with God. He replied that he felt that he had done too much wrong for God to accept him and hadn't done enough good.

"Dad, we'll never be good enough," I replied, sharing with him the message of salvation and forgiveness through Christ. I prayed and hoped that he turned to Christ before he died.

With the trial, my granddaughter's illness, the loss of our home and business, and my dad's death, I was glad to see 2011 come to an end. Prayer has always been at the center and foundation of our lives, but as a result of Bill's accident, we lost everything in the worldly sense but gained so much more. I eagerly waited to see what God had in store for us in the coming new year.

Bill and Phyllis in 2006

Phyllis with her and Bill's first grandchild in 2007

Bill with his and Phyllis's first
grandchild in 2008

Bill, home from the hospital after the
accident in September 2009

Bill and Phyllis in 2014, five years after
the motorcycle accident

A color run for charity with the family team,
kids and grandkids, 2015

Phyllis and Vanessa in 2016

Starting to cast the vision for
House of Hope NH in 2016

Chris and Rachel, Vanessa and Ben, and
Meesha and Matthew, Christmas 2017

Bill and Phyllis on their
30th Anniversary, 2017

The family and Phyllis at the 30th Anniversary celebration, 2017

Phyllis with her granddaughters in 2017

Bill and Phyllis at the New Life Home for
Women and Children Banquet, 2017

Phyllis and House of Hope NH in 2019

Granddaughter Kiyah tasting
the cookies

Bill and Phyllis 30th Anniversary 2017

Chapter 12

FOCUS
ON RECOVERY

*L*osing our home in 2011 was a tough pill to swallow. Matthew and his wife had moved back to New Hampshire after briefly living in Florida and were staying with us. They had been helping with the business and were trying to get back on their feet. Now they had to find their own place to live. There was some emotional turmoil in losing our home and having to sell or give away many of our belongings. However, it was also a relief to be in a small, one-bedroom apartment in a nice complex that had a pool. I realized I needed to rest and concentrate on taking care of Bill. Having access to a pool helped me get the physical and emotional rest I needed. The pool was good therapy for me, and I enjoyed it alone or when the kids came to visit. I even taught one of my grandkids to swim!

It was good for Bill and me to have time to focus on his recovery. His typical pattern of behavior was two bad weeks followed by a calm one. In recovery, medical professionals call it "phasing." Bad weeks consisted of Bill continually putting people down, talking without a filter, bouts of depression, and never having a pleasant or kind word for anyone, including me. Although the doctors told me what to expect and that such behavior was common for people with Bill's type of brain injury, it still wasn't what I expected. I also thought that I would handle it better. There were times I said to myself, *I don't know if I can really do this.* It was tough and seemed like something foreign had taken over Bill's body because he wasn't who or what he used to be. He was now angry all of the time and thought everyone was out to get him. In addition, his trust level in people (including me) was totally gone.

A level four brain injury made it difficult for him to have any positive thoughts. Often, I was afraid to leave him alone, plus he was in a lot of pain. At times his depression became dark and suicidal. I felt that, with such thoughts, I needed to always be with him, or have someone else around so he wouldn't act on those thoughts. Bill was on a lot of medications, but some of the meds made things worse. One drug, Remeron, seemed to have its own personality, which even the kids noticed. It worsened Bill's depression and had other side effects, so we quickly got him off of it. While there were some "mental" therapy and challenging games on the computer, he often wasn't cooperative about doing his therapy or playing those memory improvement computer games.

Bill was receiving disability payments, so we had some money coming in. God also blessed by allowing us to settle the hospital bill for far less than what we owed. Once again, we lived a bare-bones existence with rent to pay, one car, but no job. Because of Bill's condition, I was unable to work for a long time because he would have separation anxiety when I left. It was also hard for me to ask someone to watch him because he could be challenging to be around. But God was faithful in providing for our needs. We always had food on the table. Often people from church would show up at our door unannounced with a prepared meal. While Bill was legally allowed to drive, I didn't want him doing so. He would forget basic driving rules such as failing to yield, or he would drive off the road. There was always the potential for seizures. He'd had had some seizures the day of the accident and was on medication for them, but eventually got off the meds. Within six months, the seizures were no longer a problem. But I always worried they could return, especially when he was behind the wheel.

Part of my emotional healing came by becoming involved in a new ministry. I went to my pastor and told him I'd like to start a ministry to women in prison. I don't know why I wanted to be a part of this particular outreach, except that I had done similar work during my days at Youth With A Mission. I can't explain it, but I just felt called to get involved again.

With the blessing of my church, I started the prison ministry, which was the last place of obedience to God's call on my life before I was married. That time, I had run away from His calling, and this was His way of bringing me back to it. As I had a lot of time to pray, the Lord began dealing with me and softly speaking to me. After losing everything, I realized that I still had the Hope of Glory in me to give to others. I approached my pastor about starting the prison ministry, expecting him to say no!

My pastor asked me to put together a teaching series along with a description of the ministry I envisioned. After doing so, the work got approved by both the pastor and prison officials.

As I talked to others about what I thought God was laying on my heart, three women came forward and asked how they could be a part of it. I sent them to the pastor for his blessing and soon we had a team of four.

This group of women from my church began going and ministering to the prisoners at the Cheshire County Department of Corrections in Keene for one hour a week. We would typically start with prayer, occasionally sing a song, and then share one of the 13 lessons I had put together. In addition to Bible instruction, I would teach on many subjects such as overcoming bitterness, forgiveness, and many other "life" lessons. The inmates loved it when we sang and prayed with them. It gave them 45 to 60 minutes of genuine peace. They were so hungry for the love of the Lord and to feel His presence. They longed to have "something pure in this evil world," as one of them put it.

Not all of the women we ministered to gave their hearts to the Lord, but many did. The light of the Lord attracted them because darkness was a part of many of their lives. Tears were shed as healing moments came. We often thought we were going in to minister to the inmates, but we would leave saying how much God touched us. It was such an honor to serve what some would call "the least of these."

Eventually, the ministry expanded to three hours a week. I was able to do some of the lesson preparation at home while caring for Bill.

The prison ministry at Cheshire was amazing. So many women were thankful for the hope in Christ we shared with them. I told the story of my conversion, always stressing that it entailed not just a decision but a lifestyle change. "It's not just a prayer," I told them, "but a commitment to Jesus Christ."

In addition to the prisoners, we were also able to help their families and children. At one point, we assisted more than 280 women at Cheshire, helping them get into programs like Teen Challenge. "You guys are really making a difference," the guards told us in thanking us for coming. "You are the real deal," they said, encouraging us to return. We would leave feeling good about the work at the prison and the impact we were having.

Some of the stories the women shared were horrendous. One lady was incarcerated for murder after a domestic violence situation. She later wrote me a beautiful letter after being released from prison and resettling in a new area. Another lady told me her daughter was raped by her biological father during an overnight visit. This mom was locked up for drugs and theft charges.

Pouring myself into these women fed me spiritually, enriched my life, and allowed me to develop the leadership skills that I use today. It helped me to see these incarcerated women as Jesus sees them. Working in the prison ministry helped me heal from all the pain of the previous few years. Serving in this ministry meant as much to me as it did to the women I ministered to because many days assisting Bill were tough and painful. I wasn't getting much affirmation at home, but God stepped in and gave me just what I needed in that area.

Despite the Lord's encouragement, some people told me that I should go on with my life and not allow myself to be in this situation with Bill. "This isn't fair," they told me. "You're so young and so pretty." I understood that it hurt them to see me in these circumstances, but our marriage was a covenant for me. For better or worse. In sickness and in health. I took those vows seriously and refused to walk away.

What these people meant, of course, was that I should put Bill in a facility where I didn't have to deal with the day-to-day care issues. There were times that it was a tempting idea because I felt like I couldn't go on for one more day. But God reminded me from Matthew 12:20 that "a bruised reed he will not break, and a smoldering wick he will not snuff out, till he has brought justice through to victory." Bill was that bruised reed. Even today,

I realize there may come a day when I have to consider the care facility option seriously. I'm sure I will struggle with it if that day comes. Because the doctors can't predict what will happen with Bill in regards to his brain injury, I know I'll cross that bridge when I come to it. God's grace is sufficient for our needs and we take it day by day.

Bill's health has gradually improved over time, and even getting short-term relief from caring for him was a huge help. Bill's brother or my kids started coming over more and helping out. Just being able to leave for a short time was a relief for me. Plus, Bill was now able to tolerate me being gone if someone was there with him. The prison ministry helped give me a break from being a caregiver. That, along with the affirmation we got from the women that we ministered to, improved my self-esteem. It gave me a sense of purpose outside of the home.

Even years after the accident, I never know what the next day is going to hold. I might have to suddenly change my plans because every day is so different. Bill's anger still surfaces and is often directed at me. But I have to stay focused and pray to the Lord to do the work He has called me to do, especially when I'm traveling or speaking to groups.

Thankfully, I have a wonderful support group of people like my pastor, family members, and staff at our ministry home. They step into the situation when things get tough, and I have commitments to fulfill. I've learned over and over throughout my life that God's grace is sufficient. He meets the needs in every situation as I stay in His Word and prayer.

THE PREGNANCY RESOURCE CENTER

ometime in 2011, I began thinking that I needed to get a job because we were barely surviving on Bill's disability income. My daughter, Rachel, saw an ad in the newspaper for a part-time position of 10 to 15 hours a week as the director of a pregnancy resource center.

"Mom, this is perfect for you," she said. Rachel knew how much I was opposed to abortion and passionate about life. "You know the scriptures and you do ministry. This is perfect!"

"No, I can't work right now. I just can't do it," I replied, feeling that my responsibilities taking care of Bill and teaching at New Life were all I could handle. That Sunday, a lady at church mentioned the same ad to me. I took that as a sign that God was trying to tell me something. A few days later, I called the Pregnancy Resource Center (PRC), told them who I was, and about the jail and New Life ministries I was involved in.

The lady on the other end of the phone asked me my name. "Phyllis Phelps," I replied.

"Phyllis, this is Evelyn!" She was a lady who used to go to my

Bible study home group. It was the group worship meeting we held that had fallen apart after Bill's accident. I had no idea she worked at the PRC.

"I was just thinking that I can't wait to see you," she continued before knowing who I was, "and now I know why!" We had been friends for years, and I knew we would work well together. We were not only friends. She was like a sister to me, knew Bill and our situation, and could minister to me as well. God orchestrated putting another piece of the puzzle into place on my behalf.

I was hired in 2012 as the client services manager at the Pregnancy Resource Center. It was a great opportunity to minister to women facing abortion decisions and to impact their lives in a positive and Christ-honoring way. I worked at the PRC four days a week and represented them at speaking engagements on the weekends. As is true in many ministries, 10 to 15 hours a week turned into twice as many hours as women were in need at all times of the day and night.

I could write an entire book telling the stories of the woman who came to the PRC for help. They were women in various life situations seeking an abortion, including some who came in shackled by ankle bracelets. One woman who was a Christian already had five children and didn't think she could get pregnant again. Her marriage was on the rocks, so she had an affair and was pregnant as a result. She came in hoping I would confirm her decision to abort. Instead, I tried steering her toward adoption. Every week when I saw her, she wanted to go through with the abortion. Gradually, she began seeing this wasn't God's way. She eventually had the baby and gave it up for adoption, making one couple who couldn't have children very happy. I was blessed when she sent me a photo of a beautiful baby girl who was alive because of the work of the pregnancy center. This woman and her husband also went for counseling, and God eventually healed their marriage.

I got a call one night from another facility that had a girl they weren't able to help. They asked if we could talk with her, so we told them to send her over. Sariah came in and told us her story of drugs and prostitution. She said she had been with thousands of men, sobbing over what her life had become. She was now pregnant and coming to us because she thought we performed abortions.

"How can I help you?" I asked her.

"I'm not having his child. I'm aborting it. If this child is a girl, there's no way I'm bringing her into this world and into my life," she replied through her tears.

We performed an ultrasound where she saw and heard the baby's heartbeat. That procedure led her to a complete reversal, and she decided to keep her baby. Later, she accepted Christ, and I had the privilege of working with her at New Life after she completed their program. She now works with me at the current home I run as another example of God's grace, forgiveness, and restoration. Her son, Jonah, has been a blessing in both of our lives.

Once, we had a young man call the PRC pleading for us to talk to his girlfriend. She was looking to get an abortion while he was desperately trying to save his baby. He asked if she was at the PRC, but because of privacy laws, we couldn't disclose if she was at our clinic. He was distraught because, under the law, he had no voice in her decision to abort his child. My hands were tied, but I told him what I could. I later found out she was at another facility where she did abort their baby, a decision I'm sure devastated this would-be father.

Not everyone liked what we did. A schoolteacher came in to get an abortion. "Whatever you choose, we will still love you," I told her as I gently gave her the pro-life message and encouraged her to consider the life of her unborn child. She left visibly angry and had the abortion somewhere else.

Most often, I found that once women saw or heard the heartbeat of their unborn child, many changed their minds about abortion. Although I was gentle in talking with them, I stood up for protecting the unborn and speaking God's truth about life in the womb as declared in Psalm 139:19. Sadly, some women we saw had undergone as many as seven or nine abortions, using it as a form of birth control. The work at the PRC was intense with times of prayer and a lot of tears. It was a spiritual battle of life and death for the innocent. I wept for these women and their unborn babies. I prayed that God would move in their lives and reveal to me how I could help. Some of those who came to us were addicted to heroin and had been released from prison. They had nowhere to go. Often, I prayed for wisdom, and God answered.

"Lord, are you really bigger than heroin?" I asked Him one day in prayer. The drug was rampant in our community and wreaking havoc in countless lives. Almost everyone I encountered had some connection to crystal meth or heroin. While in prayer one day, I had a vision about a stream of white powder flooding the streets and a giant hand being removed from our community. God was saying, "Your nation is kicking me out. Therefore, my protection is being lifted off the land. This is one of the things I was holding back, and now it is flooding your streets." God was showing me that He was bigger than heroin and revealing to me that women caught up in this drug culture lifestyle in my community needed a place to go. These women needed Jesus Christ and the hope He offers to recover from their addiction and enslavement to drugs. It was the same help I had needed decades ago.

God tells us in Jeremiah 29:11, "For I know the plans I have for you, plans to prosper you and not to harm you, plans to give you hope and a future." That was the case for me, and working at the PRC was just a part of that plan. It was definitely God-orchestrated because He brought it together and led me in a path I couldn't see. Evelyn and I worked well together ministering life to the women who visited and giving them the pro-life message, they hadn't heard before. I continued my weekly teaching at New Life while working at PRC, speaking to women who had come out of situations similar to mine.

Shortly after I began working at the Pregnancy Resource Center, I started having an especially really rough time with Bill. He didn't want to be left alone, was miserable having me gone so much. The five hours a day I worked at the PRC seemed longer to him because he hated being alone. But his disability income wasn't enough for us to live on, so he grudgingly went along with me taking the job, but then grew to resent the time I was away from home. For the most part, my home life didn't interfere with work, but sometimes when we had to do training at night, he would call, asking me, "When are you coming home?" Often, Evelyn would intervene and calm him down.

While divorce was out of the question, I wondered if we could continue living under the same roof. The emotional outbursts, coupled with his snoring and breathing difficulties, made it hard to get the sleep I needed. Still, I knew Bill wouldn't do well in a nursing home because he would not be around the kids or me. I knew I was becoming emotionally drained. I felt wrung out like a dishrag. I needed spiritual refreshing, so I made an appointment to see Grace at New Life.

I just hoped she would have some type of answer for me or could perhaps point me toward someone who could help me with Bill's medical and behavioral issues. We met, and I left without the answers I had hoped for. I cried all the way home.

Grace did perceive that I needed recharging and invited me to attend their weekly Friday chapel just to get fed spiritually. While this wasn't really what I was looking for, I knew the two-hour round trip would give me some quiet time once a week to pray and think, which I knew would be beneficial. So, I began attending, and after about three months, Grace asked me to lead a class about women of the Bible, and share my experience with the women at New Life. I ended up teaching there for the next five years. Looking back, I can see that it gave me a different perspective and helped me build my own support network. I also learned to be kind toward the unthankful (Luke 6:35).

My teaching ministry at New Life was also the first step toward God calling me back there, although I never saw it coming. I was resistant to it because of my age. During that time, God reminded me that many people had advised me to return to New Life after my time at YWAM and how I had resisted. But as I did the homework and prepared the lessons, it was burning in me that I had to return. Now here I was, almost 30 years later, coming home. I felt like Jonah returning to Nineveh. One time, Grace reminded me about the Bible story of Job and the treasures God has in store for us through our troubles (Job 11:16). He was indeed my rock and anchor (Hebrews 6:19).

I enjoyed the challenges of balancing all these events and jobs while taking care of Bill. It was beautiful, fulfilling, and challenging. Bill was slowly healing, but we had other trials, such as when we had to put our 15-year-old dog down for medical reasons. Through it all, God was walking with me and healing me. I didn't recognize some of what He was doing until much later. I threw myself into ministry and received countless blessings, too. Over those two years, I learned a lot about going out to speak and fundraising. These things are now a regular part of my life. The gifts that were in me that had been buried for so many years began to blossom, and God was using me in ways I never imagined.

Chapter 14

TRANSITIONS

While I was working at the PRC, Bill had begun helping out with the youth at church on Monday nights. He played games with the young people, and it helped both of us. He felt wanted and needed, and I got a break from his calling the PRC looking for me.

One woman came into the Pregnancy Resource Center hooked on heroin. I knew she needed help, so I took her to New Life in Manchester, about an hour from where I lived. During that time, God reminded me of where I had come from and how New Life had been there for me when I needed it the most.

I flashed back to an incident when I was sold for the night to one or two men. I think I was about 14 or 15 at the time, and they got me drunk and gave me gifts. My sister's ex-boyfriend had asked me to come to babysit my nephew, whom I deeply loved. The men who were there (I don't know why) gave me rum and coke as soon as I arrived and plied me with as much pot and painkillers as I wanted. All of this started at about 10:00 in the morning. After drinking and drugging all day, I fuzzily remembered around supper time being introduced to an area business owner. He gave the ex-boyfriend a bonus for bringing me.

At some point, I blacked out and awoke in the morning in a strange room. After the abuse of the previous night I was a mess and in so much pain. My body would not stop shaking, and there was blood everywhere. I was sick and wanted water and a shower. I couldn't walk, and everyone was gone except the children I was supposed to be watching. I was afraid to tell anyone and so ashamed. I wanted the alcohol and the pot and to see my nephew, but I never realized the price I would pay. I was angry and never told anyone about the incident because I wasn't sure what would happen to me.

I knew that many of the girls I was seeing were coming out of the same situations and desperately needing the help I found. Even though our community is only about 100 miles from Boston, few of the girls who ended up at New Life came from that city or even New York's five boroughs. But I had been to Boston and was well aware of the reputation of the city's renown "Combat Zone," which in the 1960s was the downtown adult entertainment district and a hub of prostitution.

I knew many of the girls who got caught up in that lifestyle didn't see the red flags and needed someone to steer them in the right direction. God began quietly speaking to me about the need for a home similar to New Life in my community.

"But why me? I don't know how to do this," I protested to God. I fought and wrestled with Him, continually telling Him it was an impossible task for someone like me with no resources. At one point, I was ready to give up and said to the Lord, "I'm not Noah. I don't have 400 years. I am 50 years old. I don't want to start a home like this."

But deep in my heart, I knew this was what my community needed: A home and refuge for girls struggling and caught in the cycle of drugs, addiction, and a dangerous lifestyle. In a bargain of sorts, I told God, "You have to have my husband tell me to open the home," knowing full well Bill would never do so. There was no way he would agree to move to Manchester and spend a year at New Life while I was being trained to run a home. I think God just laughed. One day Bill came home from a prayer meeting and told me I should open a home to help the girls I saw daily at PRC. To say I was shocked when Bill agreed to the move was an understatement. This was a huge confirmation and answer to prayer. My leaders at New Life were also telling me, "Phyllis, come here and train" in preparation for such a monumental task.

I had begun working at the Pregnancy Resource Center in November 2012 and left in 2015. My teaching ministry at New Life, coupled with the increasing number of women coming in for help at PRC, was demanding more of my time and attention. I finally surrendered three years later. "If you show me what to do, I will do it, Lord," was my prayer, and I've been awed by the miracles I've seen and the doors God opened along the way.

I gave Evelyn a six month notice that I was leaving permanently to return to New Life. While I was willing to stay and train the new person, Evelyn was upset over my departure and let me leave after only one month. She hated to lose me and tried to pull me away from New Life, but I was determined to go. We had a small disagreement about the timing, but I kept telling her that God was calling me to go back to New Life. Eventually, she came to understand that, and we remain friends to this day.

After leaving, I worked a series of part-time jobs while continuing to serve in the jail ministry, at the youth ministry in our church, and attending New Life's chapel services. I also helped teach a women's Bible study before Bill and I moved into New Life, where I began working as the director in training later in 2015.

After speaking at one of the New Life banquets in 2015, I talked with Grace and told her that I felt the call to open a similar home in my area. God was tugging on my heart about the need, and she saw the opportunity as well, although she had hoped I would stay at New Life and run the new home they were opening. The original plan for my new facility was to use the "New Life" name, but we eventually decided to go in a different direction. They trained me to duplicate their work and go out and start a home on my own. I was at New Life for a full year of training and could have learned more if I had stayed longer.

During this time, I started taking on more speaking engagements. I spoke at a Right to Life event in a small town near Manchester and to The Brooklyn Tabernacle in New York on behalf of New Life. I also represented the Pregnancy Resource Center at women's retreats, Bible studies, and other engagements.

During my transition period between the Pregnancy Resource Center and New Life, the pastor who had helped us through Bill's accident and recovery also provided some emotional help and support. He has counseled us throughout our marriage and during many of the signature events in our lives. In fact, Grace sent me back to see him for counseling after I met with her. He shared the passage from Matthew 7 about building your house on the rock rather than sand. He was just one of the many people God has sent into our lives to encourage us. They have been like an army of angels surrounding us (2 Kings 6).

Chapter 15

ELIZABETH

I had just left PRC and was transitioning back to New Life when my sister-in-law, Elizabeth, began getting sick. She had joined the jail ministry team I headed and was my go-to person when a need arose. Liz and I became really close, as in best friends close. She and her husband had started coming to church with us, and we reached out to our youth pastor to help them. Elizabeth had been diagnosed with Lupus and was eventually hospitalized due to complications from the autoimmune disease. The medical professionals sent her to one of the Massachusetts General Hospital complexes in Boston, where she could get better treatment, and I insisted on accompanying them. Bill stayed home, upset with being left behind.

We got to the hospital where the smells and sounds of death were everywhere. It was very depressing and surreal. Liz was in immense pain, and so they started her on morphine. The next day, I called the church pastors and told them it was bad. Her organs had begun shutting down, but the doctors weren't telling us anything. Pastor Dave left from our church in Swanzey for the hospital while I spent time with Elizabeth in her room. After saying goodbye to her, Pastor Dave met me in the hallway. He comforted and prayed with me as I lost it emotionally. I left the hospital as he entered Elizabeth's room. He called me later to tell me she had passed.

I just didn't understand why God chose to take her only eight months after she first became ill. I loved Liz. Among her talents was that she had a way with Bill that no one else had and could reach him when no one else, including me, could.

Liz and her husband were planning on renewing their wedding vows, and we had planned a special vacation for her before she got sick. All those plans had to be canceled after she took a turn for the worse. Part of the shock of her death was that everyone thought she had about 10 more years to raise their teenage son and an older daughter. But God had other plans for the family. Sadly, her husband began drinking as part of his grieving process after her death. Shortly after that, he met another woman, and they married within six months. The family took all of this quite hard, especially him remarrying so quickly. That was especially painful for the kids.

I spoke at Elizabeth's funeral and told the audience how she came to Christ and blossomed like a rose. But inside, I was devastated and shaken by her death. After the funeral, I grieved for a couple of weeks. I had a couple of terrible days where it was hard for me to leave the house. I didn't want to talk to anyone. I had leaned on her so much during our tough times. I didn't want to face life without her. But my son helped get me out of that mindset and move on. Years later, I still cry when I think about Liz, especially on the anniversary of her passing.

God kept confirming the decision to open my own home, and New Life brought me in for a year to train as I began raising money for the home. It was my idea to only stay at New Life for one year. Grace wanted me to stay for two years to train while managing a new home they had purchased. But I knew God was calling me to start a home in my community. The feeling was so strong in my heart that I knew it was God's voice. Grace and I have a very mature relationship. Although we disagreed on the timing of my leaving, she supported me.

A group of friends and I began doing the paperwork to establish a non-profit 501(c)(3) corporation, while feeling like Noah. People would laugh and make fun of me and think I had either lost my mind or was on an ego trip. Pastor Robin Duquette from New Life Chapel was a big supporter, though, and thought my plan was from the Lord. He was the one who helped me get into New Life initially after taking me to the David Wilkerson meeting that changed my life. Pastor Duquette said he felt I was called to do this and that I needed to listen to God's voice. I initially asked to open the home under the auspices of my church. Five of us fasted and prayed one weekend about it, but it just didn't feel right at the time. So, we moved forward on our own and not under the church umbrella.

After that prayer and fasting weekend, I returned to New Life and began my training. I was raising funds for our own home, called House of Hope NH (New Hampshire), all while training and speaking for New Life. At one point, we were going to open under New Life's 501(c)(3), but their board decided against it. I think they thought it was too big of a risk, mainly because they had just opened a third home.

It was heartbreaking to be rejected as an extension of New Life because I wanted the new home to be a part of their ministry, but financially it wasn't viable. I resolved those feelings and trusted God through the process. God had a road He wanted us to follow, and we did. It was God-breathed throughout, and there were times I knew I had to get out of the way. It had been a year since I moved to New Life, and we had only raised $70,000 toward the new facility. I knew I needed so much more as well as monthly supporters. I just had to wait upon the Lord. Bill and I were about to embark on another adventure and step of faith, following where God was leading. I couldn't wait to get started!

Chapter 16

A YEAR
OF TRAINING

ill and I moved to Manchester in 2016 to begin my year of training at New Life. Saying good-bye to family was especially hard for Bill even though we were only going to be a little over an hour away. He helped load our stuff into his truck and trailer, driving it to Manchester.

Grace and the staff warmly welcomed both of us. We lived with several of the recent graduates in a house across the street from where I worked at New Life's main building. Bill would help out as well, doing maintenance and taking care of the landscaping. If he wasn't with me, a staff member would always accompany him when he was inside the main house. Most of the girls got used to seeing him, especially around mealtimes.

There were 15 women, 20 children, and eight staff members at New Life, including me. Imagine feeding more than 40 people three times a day on top of all the other ongoing daily activities! It was quite a different environment for us, especially for Bill. For one thing, we were suddenly surrounded by a lot of people.

While Bill appreciated being around others, he didn't like my hours and that I was gone a lot.

I was the first New Life graduate to be trained as a director to lead another home. I thought I was ready for this next step, but I wasn't prepared for the emotional turmoil I would experience moving back to New Life. Now I was married with children and grandchildren and had an entirely different life than when I was there three decades earlier with just my daughter. It seemed surreal to be back there because I thought New Life was a part of my past that I would never revisit.

I remembered how safe and overwhelmed I felt when I first came to New Life, and they showed me my room and bed. Returning, I experienced those same emotions all over again. It took me by surprise because I thought I had already dealt with all of them. As I walked through the different rooms, the same emotions arose from the last time I was in that same room. It was eerie. I remember again feeling "safe." Not only from a turbulent environment but from church people. I had learned that Christians have trouble accepting those who have come from rough backgrounds. It is sometimes said that Christians are the only army that shoots their wounded. I had experienced some of that. But here I was back again in my "safe" environment.

I experienced both the good memories and the pain of recovery, as well as some of the same tired, weary, and worn feelings I had 32 years earlier. I briefly flashed back to the feeling of wanting to leave. It was déjà vu, and I realized how far I had come in three decades. Bill was confused by some of my reactions. He couldn't understand why I was crying so much during the first couple of weeks and thought I missed the kids. I couldn't share a lot of details with him because I wasn't sure how he would react.

Knowing I needed time to transition, the staff left me alone for the first two weeks to acclimate. It took me the entire 14 days to readjust. Bill also struggled with his emotions as I relived all those past feelings and memories. His feelings intensified after about a month when I was well into my training, which required us to be apart. He got frustrated by the rules at New Life, living on campus, and my busy schedule. It was not a nine-to-five job and often required me to work nights, weekends, or whenever a need arose. Bill had such a rough time that he would return home to visit our grandkids every weekend. He also wanted to be with me constantly, something I couldn't do with all the training I needed. I think he resented the time I was putting in and was jealous.

Bill also didn't know my entire testimony, including the abuse I had suffered and the life choices I had made. It was a little scary as I shared my testimony and story. He learned more about the extent of the abuse but had trouble digesting it. He was hurt that I hadn't told him about some of it, but it wasn't the type of subject that came up in normal conversation. But it wasn't just Bill who didn't know all the details. I had not told a lot of people what I had been through in my life. Not even my pastor knew that I had gone through New Life's program. In fact, before Bill's accident, I hadn't talked with anyone about it. But gradually, as I shared my testimony, word got out about my experiences.

As a result of his brain injury, Bill was prone to angry outbursts. Moving to New Life saw those increase and intensify. When these eruptions happened, I had to deal with them while also continuing my training. It wasn't easy juggling it all, and this led to increased stress levels. It quickly became apparent that I would only be able to spend one year at New Life rather than the two years they recommended. Bill was tired of being there and ready to return home.

There was another factor in staying at New Life for only one year. I had begun raising money to start House of Hope in my hometown of Keene and needed to keep that effort going. In fundraising, donors generally want to see the fruits of their donations, so it's important to show progress to keep them interested in your project. So far, we had raised about $4,000. I feared that if I stayed at New Life too long, we would lose key donors that wanted to see House of Hope get off the ground. Plus, I needed to have a presence in my community due to the nature of New Englanders. We are often eager to help others in our own communities but are very wary of outsiders. As long as I was in Manchester, I was seen as an "outsider." Even though my roots were in Keene and the surrounding areas.

Cramming two years of training into one was tough, but I still remembered a lot of things from the time I lived there years ago. Ministering to the girls and interviewing them came easily to me. Because of my background, I was able to relate to them. I knew what questions to ask and how to put them at ease. I could share Christ with them and led several to the Lord. Grace included me in many meetings, and we spent a lot of time together as she taught me how to run the home like a business. She also had her assistant teach me how to write grants for funding. With the accelerated schedule, there wasn't much downtime, and I was constantly busy.

During my training, Bill would be with me at times, and he got to learn parts of the ministry but didn't travel with me to speaking engagements. Some days we would see each other a lot. However, there were other days that physical limitations such as overall weakness and migraine headaches hampered him, especially when he overdid it. At times the left side of his body would go completely numb as well. Bill did get spoiled by some of the staff members because he was the only man there. Many of them went out of their way to take care of him, which I greatly appreciated.

My daily "routine" was anything but. Each day was different, and I did everything the rest of the staff did. Some days that meant picking up donations, driving the kids to school, or lining up speaking engagements at various churches. Other days, I focused on managing the staff and settling disputes by implementing biblical principles. We taught and practiced values found in Matthew 18, such as servant leadership (verses 1-4), going in person to someone you've offended (verses 15-18), and forgiveness (verses 21-35).

Some days I'd be scheduled to do one thing and get pulled away to handle another task that came up. There was never a dull moment! My year went by quickly, and I learned a ton of skills I would use in running House of Hope NH.

One daily ritual I was able to maintain was my early morning routine. I would spend an hour in prayer, and the staff left me alone to feed my own spiritual life until about 9:00 a.m. While Bill would often sit in the living room with me, he always respected that hour and my efforts to seek the Lord.

There were many defining moments that year, such as once when a little boy was afraid and couldn't fall asleep. He was fearful because his dad would beat his mom at night. Consequently, the boy feared nighttime violence. He feared his dad or someone else would return to harm him, even though his dad was in jail. "I understand you wanting your dad, but he's sick right now and needs help," I told him.

I reassured him that no one was coming down the hallway to hurt him. I asked the Lord, "What do I do with this boy," and God answered by letting me comfort him and calm his fears until he fell asleep. "Can I just hold you for a little bit?" I asked him. It was just another confirmation that I was where I should be. God continued to bless my time at New Life as I anticipated leaving and duplicating their work at House of Hope NH.

Chapter 17

CHANGED LIVES

When I came to Christ at New Life and began living for the Lord, one of the hardest things I had to deal with was forgiveness. Forgiving my dad for abandoning me, my mom for not being there, and my stepfather for all the horrible things he had done to me. It wasn't easy to tell them I forgave them and to truly forgive. Even though he had passed away, it was tough to forgive my stepfather, and I prayed that God would help me. I went back and forth between ignoring the issue and dealing with it, but bit by bit, I worked through the anger. It was a long process, forgiving him little by little one step at a time.

I learned what the Bible says about forgiveness and that pardoning others would set me free and release me from the bondage of bitterness and unforgiveness.

For if ye forgive men their trespasses, your heavenly Father will also forgive you: But if ye forgive not men their trespasses, neither will your Father forgive your trespasses. (Matthew 6:14-15)

One of the greatest lessons I learned about forgiveness came from Matthew 18:23-35, the story about the king who forgave a debt owed to him by a servant. In contrast, the one forgiven went and found someone who owed him money and treated him cruelly. When the king heard about this, he reprimanded the man he had forgiven, calling him a "wicked servant" and turning him over to the torturers. The lesson learned was that we must forgive others, so God is free to forgive us.

I thought I had it rough, I pondered while listening to the women at New Life tell their stories. I often told them that what I went through seemed like a walk in the park compared to what they had experienced. But because of what I went through and shared with them they knew I could relate to their circumstances. God could and did use all of it for His glory.

The stories of the women who came through New Life during my one year of training could fill an entire book.

"Why should we let you come into the New Life program?" I asked one lady who sat before me during the interview process. She weighed next to nothing. "Because if you don't, I'm going to die," was her dramatic and straightforward reply.

Chills went down my spine as I remembered saying almost exactly the same thing years ago during my intake interview. Sally* reminded me of myself so long ago. She had shown up at New Life with a heroin addiction after overdosing and flatlining at the hospital. Sally was a mess, severely underweight with her hair falling out. She had already lost her brother to the same addiction. Sally became special to me as one of the first girls I interviewed as part of the intake process. God gave me a unique love for her because of all she had been through.

---

* Not her real name

After hearing her story, I felt like I was in way over my head. I was overwhelmed because I realized death was sitting right before me. I had to choose whose life I was going to help with our limited resources with Sally and the other candidates for our ministry. If I said no to Sally, she could go back out onto the streets and possibly die. We only had so many beds and the needs were so great. At times, the burden to help was overwhelming.

Wow, Lord, this is way beyond me, I thought as I prayed for guidance. *She has suffered so much more than I ever did years ago.* I felt so inadequate to meet her needs, but the Lord reminded me that He is sufficient, and it wasn't about my abilities.

And he said unto me, My grace is sufficient for thee: for My strength is made perfect in weakness. Most gladly therefore will I rather glory in my infirmities, that the power of Christ may rest upon me. (2 Corinthians 12:9)

Not that we are sufficient of ourselves to think anything as of ourselves; but our sufficiency is of God. (2 Corinthians 3:5)

I just needed to love her and share His truth, and He would do the rest—and that's exactly what happened. During one of the classes I was teaching on women of the Bible, Sally stood up while I was talking about salvation.

"Can I do that right now?" she asked, inquiring about receiving salvation through Christ. She did, standing in front of 14 people and then proclaiming, "I am a Christian now." It was a defining and pivotal moment in her life. This girl completed the New Life program and will soon graduate from college with her degree. She wants to get back into nursing, and she still keeps in touch with me. I praise God for another changed life!

One woman came to New Life after a judge ordered her into the program instead of jail. Her father had shot and killed the girl's mother before turning the gun on her. She shot him in self-defense before he could fire. She was shackled in chains when she came to us, and we immediately removed them. It was part of the process of changing her focus from shame to grace. Her original sentence was seven years, but the judge said she would only need to serve two years if she completed our program. However, if she left before finishing, her sentence reverted back to seven years. Sadly, she left the program after three months and wound up back in prison to serve her full sentence.

"I love the program and I have Jesus in my heart," she told us, "but I just can't live outside of the jail." She couldn't get used to living in a home environment and actually found prison to be more of a comfort zone.

I introduced you to Sariah in a previous chapter. She was a New Life graduate who came into the program after 20 years in the world of sex trafficking and domestic violence. I mentored her after she graduated from the program as preparation for her transitioning back into the world. Jean went on to Bible college on a scholarship and today works as my assistant at House of Hope NH.

Part of our work at New Life involved accompanying our clients when they had to go to court. At one such event, I went with Amanda, who was trying to regain custody of her son. She had received a 20-year-to-life prison sentence for producing, using, and selling crystal meth. She lost custody of her child as a result. They put me on the stand as a character witness even though her lawyer was nervous about me testifying on his client's behalf.

I spoke boldly about how her life had been transformed and that she had been clean for a year. I told the judge that I felt Amanda should get visitation rights with her son. When we left, everyone was calling me "the lion of the courtroom" because of my bold defense of her, but it was God who gave me the words to say.

Amanda was granted regular visits with her son and now has full custody of him. She realized she had to make a daily decision to live differently. To take it one day at a time, which is a common theme in nearly all recovery programs.

Sally, the lady I initially interviewed, had to return to court, and I went with her. As the trial ended, the female judge burst into tears over Sally's transformation over the past seven years she had been in the court system. The judge said that Sally had never looked so good and credited her time at New Life for the change. She ultimately ruled Sally should continue living at New Life instead of returning to jail.

It was another testament to the valuable work New Life was doing in the community as a resource for troubled women. The home had become known within the court system and as an alternative to jail. The work at New Life saved the system thousands of dollars a year by keeping women out of jail and turning them into productive members of their communities. For example, many of our own women volunteered monthly at a local food bank, giving back instead of taking from society.

The girls in our program often returned to court fearful, nervous, and stressed out, sometimes crying because it had previously been such a bad experience for them. We talked ahead of time, reminding them about how God had worked in the past in other situations. "We can't promise an outcome," we told them, "but whatever happens, God is in control."

We would prepare and teach them how to behave in court, and many exhibited genuine repentance. They had a new attitude because their hearts had been changed. It showed in the way they dressed, how they conducted themselves as well as the newfound respect they gave the judge and the judicial process. Previously, the girls may have had an "I-don't-care-you-can't-hurt-me" attitude. Now they often apologized and told the judge they were sorry for their previous behavior both in and outside of the courtroom. Most often, the girls repeatedly appeared before the same judge who had the case throughout the process.

The judges, who can spot a phony, recognized the change in these girls as they asked for mercy and accepted responsibility for their actions. Instead of portraying themselves as victims of whatever abuse they had suffered, the girls now chose to do the right thing and take responsibility for their actions. As God showed mercy, the human judges often did the same, and gave the women a second chance to turn their lives around.

It was thrilling to see women given an alternative to jail time. However, walking into court for the first time to testify was a nerve-wracking and somewhat intimidating experience for all of us. We would always take time to pray before entering the courtroom. During the girl's appearance before the judge, many of us would sit and pray in the back of the courtroom.

But after seeing God work, the next time before the judge was easier. I came to look forward to it because God always gave me the right words to say, and I trusted that the outcome for each lady was in His hands. Sometimes, God kept me from speaking altogether or saying the wrong thing. He kept me from doing things like defending the girl before the judge when she really needed to own up to her own behavior. Sometimes the judges are rough or it feels like they are biased, but I had to remember they have seen the girl more than I had. So, at times the Lord would urge me to keep quiet and not speak against the judge or the judicial process.

I'm often asked what percentage of girls who go through the New Life program actually make it. We have a saying: "If they make it the first 30 days, they make it through the program," and that pretty much sums it up. Of those who went through the entire 18-to-24-month program, about 80 percent were successful, but many people came and went. I think about half of those who initially showed up washed out within the first 30 days, many in the first week or two after beginning the program. Some had not gone through drug detox first and found it too hard to stay straight. Others did not like the Christian foundation of the program and the fact that Bible study and prayer were cornerstones of our success.

After we conducted an initial interview, the staff talked and evaluated each candidate to see if they were a good fit for the program. In fact, often during these get-acquainted sessions, we could tell if someone was a good fit and serious about turning their life around. We ran into instances where we actually ended the interview prematurely because we knew the program wasn't going to work for a particular girl. Sometimes it was tough to evaluate a candidate. We would ask them to call us back in 24 hours for our decision after we talked among ourselves and prayed for God's guidance.

It was amazing to see the New Life process at work, especially to see it as an insider. I soon realized that living there, as I had more than 30 years ago, was just the tip of the iceberg. The real work and ministry went on behind the scenes and was not always visible to the residents. I was so glad I had agreed to undergo this intensive training at New Life before venturing out to open my own home. I learned to make quick decisions such as taking a last-minute speaking engagement, and that it takes time to work through many of the processes in conducting ministry. I had only a small idea of what it took to make it all work and even today am continually learning new things.

The work at New Life was fulfilling, helping young women overcome abuse and addiction and straighten out their lives. Going to court with them and being involved in the judicial system brought back a lot of memories for me about jail and my earlier ministry there.

Chapter 18

JAIL TIME

I first became involved in jail ministry in 2011 after we lost our home and moved into a small apartment. I needed something to do but wasn't able to work full-time. I was caring for Bill after his accident and couldn't be gone the amount of time required to work a full-time job.

I felt called to be involved in this ministry because I'd had some brushes with the law earlier in my life. I had actually spent some time behind bars. My four-hour jail stint happened when I was 14, angry, and lashing out at the world.

I was so rebellious, full of hate, and did not want to follow any rules. My mom wasn't taking care of me, and I was on my own, wanting revenge for the abuse I had suffered. I was desperate to feel loved but was acting quite unlovable. "I didn't ask to be born" was my favorite saying when I was 14.

On one occasion, I disappeared from home for three days, and my mom called the police to find me. I showed up at my sister's house where I took a shower and crashed for the night. When I awoke, the house was surrounded by six police officers who took me away to jail. My sister had turned me in because she had her own issues and didn't need all my problems, too. I really didn't care that she turned me in because there were no formal charges. I was detained as a runaway, and the authorities also knew I was involved in drugs. They hoped I would tell them who was selling me the illegal substances. I was held until my parents could come and get me.

I was terrified because one particular police officer slapped me around while asking why I wasn't in school. He was an "old school" cop who was used to roughing up people, and I thought he came across like a stereotypical big city cop who didn't take any crap from anyone. He would have fit in nicely in a city like Boston, but not in our small town. This particular cop had a reputation for being coarse and mistreating people. Everyone was afraid of him, and no one ever filed charges against him or reported him. I heard that he ended up doing jail time for child abuse, but never could confirm that.

At about 90 pounds, I was so skinny that the handcuffs didn't even fit around my small wrists. It was humbling sitting in the back of a squad car and was another episode on the way to hitting rock bottom. I was angry, felt humiliated, and was deathly afraid of the police officer because he and I were the only ones in his squad car. It brought back feelings of being alone with my stepfather. I kept my eyes down in fear because I didn't know what this officer would do to me.

Even though I was scared, I pretended I wasn't afraid. In truth, I hated having my freedom taken away, and it was embarrassing when I was cuffed and hauled off to jail. It was depressing knowing that my freedom was on the other side of those bars. Part of my fear was that the police wanted me to give them the names of those who were supplying me with drugs and alcohol, which I refused to do. I never did squeal because I was afraid for my life and the lives of those I loved. I knew the drug dealers would come after us if I ever gave them up.

I knew I could relate to many of the women who were in jail. So, a group of us created the prison ministry with the idea of teaching biblical concepts and ministering to the women. The topics I developed ranged from the story about the woman at the well (John 4), teachings on the parables of Christ, and a lesson on God's faithfulness. I also developed messages about salvation, such as the story of Nicodemus found in John 3. All of the teachings contained a lot of scriptural references and focused on Jesus being the one way to heaven.

Before beginning the formal jail ministry, we had to attend classes about what we could and couldn't do inside, what happens during a lockdown, and other behavioral procedures. We also had to be taught about prison culture and what to expect. For example, we were told not to give the prisoners any items, share any personal information, or even talk about ourselves.

We learned that prisoners at Cheshire Correctional were housed on the mezzanine level. There was also a common area, as well as solitary confinement. We were told we couldn't wear the color red because it was thought that red incited violence among the inmates. Going to the men's area of the prison freaked me out, and I started shaking all over because I was intimidated by them. It may have been because of my past experience with men, but to this day, I'm not sure why my body reacted this way. However, I was fine on the women's side.

Once we were admitted, the guards let us walk around the yard and common area. We began spreading the word among the inmates about the new Bible studies that were starting and asking the women if they wanted to attend. Many signed up, but some taunted the inmates who expressed an interest in us. Most who attended got along with each other and us, although they knew they had to watch what they said in the room. Only once did I have to ask someone to leave because they were being verbally disruptive, by trying to provoke an argument among inmates, changing the subject, and getting off-topic.

Despite the atmosphere and company, I wasn't afraid to give them orders and demonstrate that I was in charge. I found that the inmates respected that. We ended up having about nine of the 31 inmates at Cheshire attend. Many were hungry to hear about Christ and salvation. For most of them, it was a good break from the prison routine, and a chance to do something "normal."

As we got to know the ladies, many of their stories were heart-breaking, and I could relate to what they were going through. Some of them came from homes where drug abuse was rampant, or steeped in the drug culture. Many would have to return to that environment after they got out of prison because there were few if any homeless shelters and halfway houses available for them. Most inmates chose to go back to their old stomping grounds, some with tears in their eyes. They thought they had little choice, even though I would try to introduce them to Teen Challenge and other programs to give them other options after they were released.

Most of the inmates were incarcerated for minor offenses. However, one lady had committed murder by running over her boyfriend with a car. She struggled with feeling the Lord couldn't forgive her for such a crime, but she ultimately came to the Lord in prison. She was later transferred to another facility and wrote a heartfelt letter telling me how much she appreciated our team coming to help them. She was later released, and the last I heard was doing well.

Another prison inmate had a big scar stretching from her lip to the side of her cheek. Her boyfriend, who was in a gang, had discarded her but said he didn't want anyone else to have her, so he cut her beautiful face. She told me that despite the pain and the turn her life had taken, she was thankful to be in jail because she found Jesus there. "I should be dead," she told me, "but the reason I'm here is because of Jesus. That's where He met me."

She eventually was transferred elsewhere and I haven't heard from her since. Her story, and many others, really touched my heart. I always thanked the women for sharing with me and letting me in on their pain. "I could be where you are, but for the grace of God. I just didn't get caught," I told the ladies. As I related my story, they saw what I meant. I had made a lot of the same bad choices they had, but somehow, except for my four hours in jail, had escaped the long arm of the law.

In a strange twist of fate, I knew one of the inmates at Cheshire from my previous life. We had met on the streets and our initial rivalry was over a boy. She was dating him and one day he and I were getting high when she showed up. I had no idea he was with her. He never let on to me, either, so she was angry at me, and I was mad at the boy for putting me in that spot. From that day on, she and I were enemies. One time at 2:00 in the morning, my sister and I pulled over and began harassing her. I badly wanted a piece of her.

But when we met in prison, I asked for forgiveness over how I had treated her. She forgave me, and we both cried. She eventually came to know the Lord as well, but her story didn't have a happy ending. "I'm not going to make it on the outside, Phyllis," she told me one day while weeping. I asked her to call me when she got out and I'd help her. Instead of doing so, she called her drug dealer and wound up dying from a heroin overdose.

Many of the women we encountered were angry and resentful over life's circumstances and how they landed in jail. Some were like I was at 14, mad at and lashing out at the world. Their pain was all they had. While I never asked them what they were in prison for, many would tell me anyway. Instead, I would ask them, "What got you here, meaning what bad choices did you make? Have you thought about the choices you made that landed you here?" Some of them had gotten into situations they wanted to get out of but didn't know how. Others were threatened by current or former boyfriends or drug dealers. Many of these girls committed crimes while in those flawed relationships. They didn't know how to walk away or make the relationship-crime cycle stop. Many were afraid to do so because of the fear of retaliation from those who threatened them. I could relate, having been in similar situations.

Some of the lady prisoners attended our Bible studies because it looked good on their records, especially if they were up for parole. Others owned up to the choices they had made in life and refused to become victims. Some truly repented, especially after hearing about God's love and the forgiveness available in Christ. Many of them were hungry for love and had made bad choices in life as a result. They got involved with the wrong kind of men and paid the price for their poor decisions. Among the inmates, there was a saying that "a bad boyfriend is way worse than a bad drug," and in many cases, it was that bad boyfriend that led to them being in jail. Many of these women were desperate, so thirsty for love and acceptance that they drank up God's love and were ready to hear the salvation message. They were like a dry, parched desert landscape thirsty for the refreshing water of life. It always amazed me that many of these women weren't churched and were blown away by the simple message that "God is love." I could see Jesus in some of them, despite their circumstances and the things they had done.

Through the years, God has blessed the jail ministry,

allowing me to speak to hundreds of women. I helped our team put together the first monitored visiting program in our area so children could see their incarcerated parents. I'm constantly reminded of the message found in Matthew 25:36: "I was in prison and ye came unto me." As I've continued serving in the prison ministry, I am blessed by seeing God work miracles in the lives of so many in need of Christ and His redemption.

Chapter 19

THE IMPORTANCE
OF MENTORING

I have had a lot of help along my journey from recovery to starting my own home for women in need. At the top of the list of those God has sent my way is Grace Rosado, who has been a friend and mentor since I first showed up on the doorsteps of New Life Home for Women and Children in January 1984.

Grace was the first one to show me God's unconditional love. She just glowed and was full of the Lord's love. I wanted what she had. When I first walked into New Life, she welcomed me and took me in like a mother receiving a wayward child. She became like a second mother to me, skilled at explaining things in a hands-on way that made sense.

For example, when I first arrived at New Life, one of the chores we were required to do was wash dishes. I hated it! But Grace came alongside and helped me. "I enjoy doing dishes," she explained. "This is my time where I think about the Lord and meditate on Him." This had a profound effect on me as I learned to utilize that time to meditate on God's Word and pray while getting work done. I came to cherish that "God time" and now teach the girls I mentor the same thing as I help them with their tasks. "You know," I tell them, "the morning chores are that time you can set the tone for the day." Grace showed so much of Christ's love toward me, especially when I had a bad attitude. I remember one time not knowing how to iron clothes and feeling sorry for myself. Grace simply told me she loved me. It was like Jesus Himself was looking into my eyes and telling me He loved me.

While Grace reflected Christ's love toward all of the girls at New Life, at the same time she was never naïve about our behavior. She was a disciplinarian and had the uncanny ability to walk through the house and instantly know if something was off. She was always right in her assessment of what was going on! For example, she could immediately spot if we had a bad attitude, were gossiping, or if someone was trying to sneak chocolate donuts out of the freezer in the middle of the night. We learned not to speak against those in authority over us, but to be unified with them. She would correct us in love but was firm in her guidance and discipline. And, for the record, that someone sneaking chocolate donuts was me. Eventually, they put a lock on the freezer and that was the end of my midnight raids!

Grace also taught me to spend an hour every morning with the Lord before starting the day, something I continue doing today. We learned the principle of the Bible, utilizing Teen Challenge material to learn essential life lessons. Ironically, when I first arrived at New Life, I thought the routine was very strange because the curriculum was Bible, Bible, Bible.

We were taught to utilize Matthew 18:15-17 to confront people and resolve issues. That scripture refers to talking to a person one-on-one, then taking a friend along if the one-on-one doesn't work, and finally telling a broader audience. I learned that clearing the air is definitely needed before prayer because holding a grudge against another person blocks our communication with God, according to Matthew 5:22-25 and Mark 11:25-26. Grace taught me that when the battles come, we should fast, pray and wait for God to act.

Grace has had such an impact on me that Bill once said he thought I could be her daughter because I took on her sayings, mannerisms, and even her love of the King James Version of the Bible.

George Rosado has also been a great friend and mentor. He came out of the drug culture, went through the Teen Challenge program, and became friends with Nicky Cruz, a former gang leader turned evangelist. Cruz wrote about his conversion in the book, "Run Baby Run." His conversion was depicted in the 1970 film, *The Cross and the Switchblade,* starring Erik Estrada as Cruz and Pat Boone as Teen Challenge head, David Wilkerson. George filled the role of pastor at New Life, but would often eat dinner with us while encouraging all of the girls to be faithful and true to the Lord. He would also help out in the office or just come by and play video games with us.

George was also great at holding us accountable. His favorite saying was, "always tell the truth." My natural go-to was to avoid dealing with my issues. I would opt to work and find more tasks to throw myself into, rather than confront what I needed to deal with. George saw right through this tactic and would often say to me, "Work isn't always the answer."

George functioned as a father figure, too, but could be very strict, rebuking us in love when we needed it. One time he was speaking at a Mennonite church and a group of us girls went along to meet people and share our testimonies. During the service, I dropped the full offering plate as it was passed during a quiet moment. George was furious and his face turned red. I was so embarrassed as we scrambled around to pick up all the money. Later we laughed about it, but at the time, I could have died!

While he could be strict, he also taught us to be thankful for everything that came our way. I remember one time there was nothing to eat. He came in and told us to pray that we would get our favorite food. *Okay, I'll do this,* I thought because I knew it wasn't going to work. *I'm not going to get my favorite food.* I prayed for hot dogs and beans, and sure enough, someone delivered hot dogs and beans to us! I was dumbfounded because I never expected it to happen. But it was a great lesson about praying in faith that has stayed with me these many years later.

I remember when I first started collecting funds to open House of Hope NH, George asked me, "How much money do you have?"

"Pastor George, I only have $500," I replied.

"You need to be thankful for that $500," he responded in a gentle rebuke. "You need to thank God for every dollar you get toward that home. If it's of the Lord, He will provide."

Even today, I don't get afraid when funds get low, but I pray in faith, a lesson I learned from George. He always said, "Words are cheap. We need to see it [faith] in your life. We need to show love, not talk [about] it." When funds are low and we need money for something else at the home, I think of his words and tell my board, "We've been here before, and God always comes through." I've learned that God faithfully provides for our needs, but not necessarily on our timeline. The faith lesson is simple: If we had the money in the bank, we wouldn't pray and depend upon the Lord, but He provides when we ask, seek, and knock. (Matthew 7:7-8) Such walking by faith keeps us humble and depending upon Christ, and not relying on our own strength or cunning.

George and Grace have been in my life for more than 30 years and remain mentors and great friends.

In addition to the Rosados, I've been blessed to have mentors from Youth With A Mission, especially Doug and Deb Tunney. Traveling all over the world ministering to others, they have been mentors and big supporters of House of Hope NH.

Pastor David Berman walked with both of us through Bill's accident. He was instrumental in helping me start the jail ministry, giving me advice, and being straightforward with me about what to expect and how to best minister to the inmates. He often told me things I didn't want but needed to hear.

Pastor Jim Cymbala from Brooklyn Tabernacle has had a big impact on me through his preaching and Bible study videos. "Glorify Christ, not man or the home," Pastor Cymbala once said, and that stuck with me. Today, when I have the ladies share in a church environment, I tell them to glorify Jesus and not House of Hope. Our ladies reflect that glory as they study the Bible and live for Christ, but sometimes we have to start at the very beginning. "Oh, I've been a Christian for so many years," a new girl may tell me when I first meet her, yet she may not even know how to look something up in the Bible. So, I watch how they interact with the Bible, and many times they may have said a prayer, but didn't know the Savior or have not been properly discipled.

Two other men of God have helped mentor me through the years.

Pastor Robin Duquette, who I've known for a long time, was the one who took me to see David Wilkerson in Manchester and brought me to George and Grace at New Life. He has continued to encourage and mentor me through every adventure.

Pastor Matt Worrall has been in our area for many years. He's been a huge supporter and encourager and immediately got behind the idea of a home here in Keene. He has a knack of calling or texting me at just the right time with a word of encouragement. He once told me that when you are in ministry, people won't always be thankful. Nevertheless, we must continue serving others because we are really doing it for the Lord (Matthew 25:40, Hebrews 6:10).

I've also been helped by many people associated with Teen Challenge and have utilized their material in discipling countless women over the years. My mentoring journey included stops at New Life and Youth With A Mission, along with the influence of many people at Teen Challenge. I've also been helped by, and had good relationships with, many pastors in our area over the years. I am grateful for each person God has brought into my life to share in my journey.

Chapter 20

HOUSE
OF HOPE NH

O ur new governing board got together in 2017 at the end of my training year, and we started fund-raising like crazy. We had an ambitious goal of $250,000 but trusted God to provide if it was His will for the home to open.

Our board consisted of friends, a pastor and his wife, and several others. All of them had helped pray for and raise funds for the ministry. They all believed in the vision of the home and helped me with numerous fundraising projects. We were able to raise about $90,000 from these events, including yard sales, a banquet, a golf tournament, and an auction. Several businesses in our community helped with the latter by donating goods and services. I was also speaking in churches and sharing our vision. As a result, several area churches began supporting us as people saw the need and decided to help.

Pastor Gary Wilkerson helped connect me with some resources, including several people from New England Teen Challenge, who offered to help with our training. Beth Greco from the Hoving Home in Garrison, New York was particularly generous, offering to assist us anyway she could.

We started looking at properties and found a beautiful home, originally priced at $650,000. It was way out of our price range, but the housing market was collapsing as we were looking to buy a house to fit our needs. Because of the weak housing market, the price had dropped to $399,000. That was still above the average home price in our area. As my pastor's wife and I prayed, I knew that this was the house we were supposed to have, but we had almost no money.

Despite our successes, we were a long way from our goal, and I was getting discouraged. One day a close friend invited me to breakfast for my birthday but I couldn't go because I was so sick and weary. *What am I going to tell the board, my pastor, and all of those who have gotten behind us financially?* I wondered. The following Monday, my friend and I got together for breakfast. She handed me a check for $265,000 for the home. The donor couple wanted to remain anonymous, and I knew this was God's answer to what we needed to purchase a property for our group home. God again showed me that what is impossible for man is possible for Him (Luke 18:27).

The $265,000 gift was a turning point for us. Right about the time the funds came in, our 501(c)(3) was approved, marking another example of God's perfect timing. The couple donating the funds were liquidating another non-profit and had to give the funds to another 501(c)(3). They knew Bill and me, believed in what we were doing, and saw the need in our community. As I was looking at and praying about the house, I thought was perfect for us, the $265,000 donation came in and the doors opened up for us to buy it.

Another sign from God was that the local zoning board

voted 5-0 to approve our establishing a home in our community. The unanimous approval from them was a big deal because many people didn't want a group home of any kind in their neighborhood. But the board voted to approve converting the house into a group home, and we cleared another hurdle. Once again, God's timing was perfect because right after we bought the home, the housing market rebounded, and prices soared. We would have never gotten this home at any other time.

The house was in pretty good condition but needed a few things done to it, such as minor repairs to the windows, painting, and similar small projects. The bedrooms were nicely done, and each room had a different theme to it. A ship's captain had returned from war in 1777 and built the house. It is a small farmhouse and has that historical look and feel to it, which we have worked to preserve. The house even has a full basement and cold cellar, which was a delightful addition. We had the option to designate it as a historic landmark, but that would mean opening it up to the public. That is something we can't do for the safety of our ladies. Like many New England properties, the 200-plus-year-old house had some of the original exposed beams and cast iron. It was drafty and cold and needed weatherproofing as many of the older homes in our area did. We also had to make other modifications, such as installing a sprinkler system. In addition to the house, we have a lot of land, trees, and tons of potential to expand and utilize what God has given us as the ministry grows.

We took possession of the house on Pearl Harbor Day, December 7, 2018, and moved in the next day. In retrospect, I should have waited to do more cleaning and preparing the home before moving in. However, we were so excited by God's provision that we couldn't wait to get started! Our first staff members began moving in three weeks later on December 29.

Despite the wonderful blessing of getting the house, I realized it is just that. A facility to house ladies in need. The real work of the ministry is done by the people that have come alongside us.

In addition to our board members, we have been blessed with an incredible staff and leadership. Spiritual Director, Reverend David Berman, has been my pastor since 2005 and is the senior pastor of the Christian Life Fellowship Church in Swanzey. His extensive ministry experience includes church planting, training theological students, mentoring, and consulting. He also has vast experience in business and media. Pastor Berman is a terrific asset to our ministry because he knows how substance abuse contributes to the downward spiral in relationships as well as every other aspect of life. He knows this firsthand as one who was an addict during his teenage years. As a pastor, he is no stranger to dealing with the most difficult problems resulting from addiction. Irresponsible and other self-destructive behaviors are common traits among addicts.

"I have been an addict, I know what it feels like, I know the hopelessness, I know the pain, and I know exactly what it does and how to get free," he tells the girls we work with. As a spiritual counselor, Reverend Berman has helped hundreds of people transform their lives by embracing the biblical principles he teaches. Because he's been there, he can cut through the façade many of our girls put up and get right to the root causes of their addiction. Most of all, he reaches out to them with the love of Christ, offering them the spiritual hope they need to break free of addiction.

Jessica Stevens, our administrative assistant, has a passion for women who are struggling to overcome life-controlling issues. Her own personal experiences allow her to be effective in the ladies' recovery and future plans. Jess had been volunteering with us and initially came on board as our computer whiz. She approached me one day and said she felt called to come work at the home. She sought counsel from her pastor who agreed that it was a good fit for her. After much prayer, Jess became more involved and eventually left a job with good benefits to come help us. Since then, she has shown herself to be a real asset to our work and someone I count on as my right-hand woman. Jess has a wonderful love for the Lord and a knowledge of His Word that guides her daily. Jess works in the office, organizes, plans, schedules, and manages communications. She keeps the home's schedule steady and on track, manages the scheduling of staff and volunteers, and coordinates our speaking engagements.

My daughter-in-law, Lateesha Phelps, has a background in early childhood education and teaching. Lateesha grew up in foster care and moved around a lot because her mom had addiction issues. Bill and I led her to the Lord when she was 17 and took her in. She is like a daughter to me. Lateesha is a real people person who just loves helping others and has a passion for seeing women overcome their challenges. At House of Hope, she helps keep the ladies on schedule with their classes, assists the staff with special projects, spends time cooking in the kitchen, and helps out wherever there is a need. Lateesha works three days a week in the home and helps keep me organized by tracking all the clothes and other items people donate.

Staff Assistant Jean Davis is a graduate of New Life, and works as a volunteer with House of Hope. She keeps the ladies on their nighttime and weekend routines and assists with cooking responsibilities while finishing her college degree. As our "house mom," Jean came on board after initially telling me she "wasn't called" to come help me. Jean was speaking at various churches around the area when she called me up one morning out of the blue. "I feel called to come help you," she told me. Jean and I met while I was at PRC and she was finishing up at New Life. Jean was enrolled at a local Bible college and praying for direction after transitioning out of New Life, but they didn't hire her. She called me while working odd jobs and said she "couldn't shake the feeling" that she should come work with me. I felt all along Jean was called to help me, but she had to be convinced by the Lord and stop fighting it. Sounds familiar! Jean has since become my Timothy, Aaron, and Ruth and is a real prayer warrior. She is someone who came along and became a trusted right hand and valuable asset.

We officially opened House of Hope NH in March 2019 and took in our first resident after getting the staff trained and settled. As I write this, we are housing three girls and have a monthly budget of about $8,600. Presently, we can only have three residents because we are still working on bringing the house up to code. Ultimately, we will house 12 girls at our Keene home with a yearly budget of about $148,000. We hope to have four full-time staff members in addition to myself. That's our board's vision to meet the needs of women in crisis in the Monadnock region of southwestern New Hampshire.

We had planned to have a grand opening sometime in Spring 2020, depending on how the work proceeded after slowing down this past winter. However, with the COVID-19 crisis, that plan got delayed indefinitely. Many people in our community are watching to see how it goes and if the bottom falls out for me. But God is faithful. He has provided people to help, businesses to donate labor and materials, and much more. God has called me to this work, and He will see that it succeeds.

As we continue to work on the house and establish House of Hope NH, the work of ministry continues. I recently went to court with one girl who was facing multiple years in jail but ended up getting 30 days probation because she is living at House of Hope. Because God went before us, she walked out of the courtroom feeling blessed with a new lease on life and a second chance.

I now see that God is using the pain and suffering I endured early in my life to help me connect with and minister to others. He has healed and strengthened many women and children through New Life and now House of Hope. I believe God will use our work to impact this next generation for Christ! We are just beginning this new adventure as God leads us day by day and moment by moment.

Chapter 21

THE GOOD SAMARITAN

The Bible forms the basis of our ministry and one of my favorite Scripture passages is Luke 10:25-37. It is the familiar story of the Good Samaritan:

And, behold, a certain lawyer stood up, and tempted him, saying, Master, what shall I do to inherit eternal life? He said unto him, What is written in the law? how readest thou? And he answering said, thou shalt love the Lord thy God with all thy heart, and with all thy soul, and with all thy strength, and with all thy mind; and thy neighbour as thyself. And he said unto him, Thou hast answered right: this do, and thou shalt live. But he, willing to justify himself, said unto Jesus, And who is my neighbour? And Jesus answering said, A certain man went down from Jerusalem to Jericho, and fell among thieves, which stripped him of his raiment, and wounded him, and departed, leaving him half dead. And by chance there came down a certain priest that way: and when he saw him, he passed by on the other side. And likewise a Levite, when he was at the place, came and looked on him, and passed by on the other side. But a certain Samaritan, as he journeyed, came where he was: and when he saw him, he had compassion on him, and went to him, and bound up his wounds, pouring in oil and wine, and set him on his own beast, and brought him to an inn, and took care of him. And on the morrow when he departed, he took out two pence, and gave them to the host, and said unto him, Take care of him; and whatsoever thou spendest more, when I come again, I will repay thee. Which now of these three, thinkest thou, was neighbour unto him that fell among the thieves? And he said, He that shewed mercy on him. Then said Jesus unto him, Go, and do thou likewise.

Neither the Samaritan nor the innkeeper asked what nationality the injured man was or what manner of life he was living. The innkeeper took him in, tended to his wounds, fed him, clothed him, and gave him a warm bed.

I believe that God has called House of Hope NH to be the inn where Good Samaritans can bring the wounded and those left for dead by the thief who comes to rob, kill, and destroy. We take in women from all walks of life and every income level. We charge them nothing for our services because drugs and their lifestyles have left them without any resources. For most of them, their poor choices have destroyed their health and relationships.

Why do we do this? It is because of the need as outlined in Mark 2:16-17, another Scripture passage I use to educate others about our ministry:

And when the scribes and Pharisees saw him eat with publicans and sinners, they said unto his disciples, How is it that he eateth and drinketh with publicans and sinners? When Jesus heard it, he saith unto them, they that are whole have no need of the physician, but they that are sick: I came not to call the righteous, but sinners to repentance.

I think back to an experience I had during my time at Youth With A Mission. We traveled to Massachusetts, and after one of our drama skits in Boston, were instructed to pair up and share Christ's love with those we met. I saw a man much older than me. He was a street person, dirty, and had a long beard with vomit in it. He would not look up or make eye contact with anyone. I broke the ice by commenting about the beautiful park. He just nodded without saying a word, and I began talking about how God's creation was made for mankind's pleasure. He just quietly nodded. Then I asked him, "Can we pray for you?"

"Yes," he replied.

As we were praying, I felt I should hug him. *No way, I simply can't*, I thought. *He smells like vomit and what if he has lice?* In my mind I argued against hugging him, but when we stopped praying, I saw a tear roll down his face. I immediately hugged him and he began weeping.

"What's wrong?" I asked.

"I haven't been touched by another person in seven years," he replied. I never forgot that day or the power of a simple hug. Everyone has a story, and we never know the impact we can have with just a kind word or deed.

The girls who come to us are sick, beaten down by life, addiction, and poor choices. Many come from the towns outside of Boston and area homeless shelters. They have nothing and have lost all hope. We share the good news of new life in Christ with them and the promise that they can have a fresh start.

We utilize a three-step program at House of Hope to help women transform their lives. By the time they get to us, most of them have burned all bridges and have nothing but the clothes on their back and maybe a bag or backpack. During their first month, the ladies get acclimated to their surroundings and into a new and healthy routine. We introduce them to the concept of living by faith and offer them the stability in their lives that they haven't had. They get three meals a day, a first for many of them.

The girls who come to us pay $500, which we deposit into an account for incidentals or medical care that isn't covered by Medicaid and in case they need it in the future. If they decide to leave us, they get the money back so they can get home. If they stay, the money remains deposited to meet the many needs that will come up. There are no additional charges for them to stay with us.

After 30 days, we meet with each lady, asking if they would like to commit to going through our entire 12- to 18-month program. We must determine if they are a good fit for us. In turn, they must decide if they want to change and go in a different direction. From there, the women who stay work on three short-term and three long-term goals.

The short-term goals include helping each lady get a driver's license or state identification, straightening out any court issues, and nurturing them back to health. Our long-term goals include education (including computer skills) as well as working toward securing housing once they leave our program. We also help reunite them with their children if that is an issue.

We put our ladies on a schedule that includes classes and learning job skills. Together, we come up with a plan for parenting and finances. During their stay with us, the women learn how to manage relationships, finances, and their homes according to God's design.

Our goal for each graduate is the same: To help them get a job, a vehicle for transportation, and housing. Once our girls graduate from the program, they can return at any time for ongoing maintenance. They can also contact me whenever they need help coping with the stress or temptations to return to the old lifestyle. We attempt to build a family environment, and we hope many girls will return to participate in events we are having. That is what happened at New Life and what we hope to replicate here. We also get them into a church and help each girl build a support system within their church family and with others walking in the Christian faith. For example, one of our girls is working for us part-time on the night shift and will eventually get a job as a bank teller when she graduates. We'll work on getting her a vehicle and toward reuniting her with her six-year-old daughter.

Everywhere I speak, I distribute fliers and tell others about the work of House of Hope NH. Speaking engagements are vital as a part of raising the funds we need to support this work. We do not take any state or federal funding, so we rely on grants, fundraising, and monthly donors. Most of the time I take several girls with me when I present the ministry at a church, and I typically have one of the girls speak as well.

I love sharing about the work we are doing and the needs we have. But when people hear from the ladies themselves and how they are working to turn their lives around, it makes a more significant impact. One time I took a girl with me (let's call her Anne) who came to us from Arkansas after hearing about House of Hope NH from her grandmother, who lives in our area. Anne began calling me regularly for about six months before she came here. At our speaking engagement, she told the church gathering, in her pronounced Southern accent, "Every time I'd call, Miss Phyllis would ask, 'Would you like me to pray for you?' And I'd always say, 'Yes, Ma'am!'" As a result of Anne's testimony, we were able to raise several thousand dollars in support and got two monthly donors. Praise God for His faithfulness!

In addition to those supporting us, many people generously volunteer their time and talents, pouring their lives into these ladies. These volunteers desire to see our girls set free from the grip of sin and destruction. For example, we have a sewing teacher who comes in and shows our ladies how to sew and do crafts. As I speak at churches and with people I come into contact with, I'm able to find volunteers.

House of Hope NH is up and running, but our work is just beginning. We have a long way to go in restoring lives. Here in New England, the need is so great. Just a few weeks ago, two teens, ages 13 and 14, overdosed, and the 13-year-old died. A grandmother brought her teen granddaughter to visit us, but the girl wound up back to the streets. She later overdosed on drugs and died. She had wanted to become a veterinarian but now is gone forever.

Our small town, 100 miles from Boston and two hours from New York, is being devastated by drugs. Jeremiah 9:21 speaks about death coming to our streets and homes to "cut off the children from without, and the young men from the streets." That is the reality of what is happening in New England. It is what we face every day in trying to rescue as many as we can and turn them to the Lord. Only He can save them and snatch them from the one who wants to destroy their lives.

Recently, we had an inspector come through the house as part of the process of getting a permit. He was amazed at what God is doing here. "Wow, it's like this house was built for what you're trying to do here. I hope you flourish."

He saw God moving through the home and the work we are doing at House of Hope NH. I hope as you've read my story and followed my journey, you'll be encouraged that God is working in the lives of those who turn to Him for salvation and hope. God restored my life and gave me a new purpose and dream. He can and will do the same for you as you turn to Him.

Afterword

*H*ouse of Hope NH is a new work, raised up by the Lord for such a time as this (Esther 4:14). Our message is simple, and based on the timeless message of God's love found in John 3:16.

For God so loved the world, that he gave his only begotten Son, that whosoever believeth in him should not perish, but have everlasting life.

The girls who come to us need the love and hope that only God can give. But we can't do it alone.

As I write this, we are housing three girls and have a monthly budget of about $8,600. Ultimately, we will shelter 12 girls at our Keene home with a yearly budget of about $148,000.

Our board of seven men and women is committed to "Saving Lives, Impacting Generations" through this non-profit work. They are involved in our fundraising and grant writing efforts as we seek those to come alongside us to maintain this ministry. In addition, we ask businesses, churches, and individuals to partner with us monthly to maintain the ministry. Our partners help us reach more women and children with the life-changing message of hope in Jesus Christ.

We ask you to consider helping us. For just $5.00 a month, the cost of two cups of coffee, you can make a difference in the lives of countless women and children. Your gift of any amount helps us feed, clothe, and house these women so they can heal from their trauma and abuse in a safe and Godly atmosphere. We are in the business of Saving Lives and Impacting Generations.

We welcome your input and donations. Visit us at: houseofhopenh.org, or send your gift to:

House of Hope NH
P.O. Box 10371
Swanzey, NH 03446
May God bless you as you reach out to help others.

About the Author

*P*hyllis Phelps is married with three adult children and eight grandchildren. She is the founding director of House of Hope NH along with Bill, her husband of 32 years.

Through her own personal testimony, she shares the love of Jesus Christ, faith, and hope. Phyllis graduated from New Life Home for Women and Children in 1984 and Youth With a Mission in 1985. Since 2012, Phyllis enjoyed many opportunities to teach and volunteer at New Life Home. She completed an intense director's training program under New Life's leadership team in 2017. Phyllis has led a women's jail ministry since 2011 and served on the Gen Now youth team for six years as well. She has been an active member at Christian Life Fellowship since 2005. Phyllis' vision, along with her husband Bill, is to bring hope to those suffering with life controlling issues through a long-term residential program located on 5.5 acres in Keene, Hew Hampshire.

House of Hope NH opens its doors for women and their children to experience freedom in Christ in a warm and loving atmosphere.